Mastering NetScaler V. X

Learn how to deploy and configure all the available features of Citrix NetScaler® with the best practices and techniques you need to know

Rick Roetenberg

Marius Sandbu

BIRMINGHAM - MUMBAI

Mastering NetScaler VPX™

First published: November 2015

Production reference: 1161115

Published by Packt Publishing Ltd.
Livery Place
35 Livery Street
Birmingham B3 2PB, UK.

ISBN 978-1-78528-173-0

www.packtpub.com

Notice

Credits

Authors
Rick Roetenberg

Marius Sandbu

Reviewer
Yugandhar Ananda

Commissioning Editor
Dipika Gaonkar

Acquisition Editor
Harsha Bharwani

Content Development Editor
Sumeet Sawant

Technical Editor
Tanmayee Patil

Copy Editors
Stephen Copestake

Vikrant Phadke

Project Coordinator
Shweta H Birwatkar

Proofreader
Safis Editing

Indexer
Tejal Soni

Graphics
Jason Monteiro

Production Coordinator
Aparna Bhagat

Cover Work
Aparna Bhagat

About the Authors

Rick Roetenberg is a technical consultant at ITON ICT in the Netherlands. He has more than 5 years of experience in implementing products available from Citrix, especially networking products. He is also responsible for pre-sales with customers at ITON ICT. Recently, he succeeded the Citrix Networking for Datacenter Specialist Practicum. Rick has also presented at DuCUG, the Dutch Citrix User Community, where he explained that NetScaler is more than just an ICA proxy. He has always had a lot of interest in technology, and his current focus is on Citrix network products.

Rick posts blogs at www.rickroetenberg.com, where he shares more information about Citrix's products and all that is necessary in addition to these products. He can be contacted at rick@rickroetenberg.com. His Twitter handle is @rroetenberg.

Marius Sandbu is a senior consultant from Norway. He has over 10 years of experience in IT. He has worked as an architect and instructor at Veeam, Microsoft, and Citrix. He has also presented at the NetScaler master class and been to local Citrix user groups' events. Marius is the author of other NetScaler books as well, including *Implementing NetScaler VPX™, Packt Publishing*.

He is also a Microsoft MVP, Veeam Vanguard, and PernixPro.

Marius posts blogs on https://msandbu.wordpress.com/, where he shares information from the software-defined space. He can be contacted at msandbu@gmail.com or on Twitter at @msandbu.

About the Reviewer

Yugandhar Ananda works as a Citrix consultant. This has helped him get good exposure to Citrix technologies, real-time issues with production servers, XA/XD/PVS, and NetScaler.

He is a quick learner and can easily adopt new technologies, which is his strength. His hobbies are making new friends and reading new technical articles.

www.PacktPub.com

Support files, eBooks, discount offers, and more

For support files and downloads related to your book, please visit www.PacktPub.com.

Did you know that Packt offers eBook versions of every book published, with PDF and ePub files available? You can upgrade to the eBook version at www.PacktPub.com and as a print book customer, you are entitled to a discount on the eBook copy. Get in touch with us at service@packtpub.com for more details.

At www.PacktPub.com, you can also read a collection of free technical articles, sign up for a range of free newsletters and receive exclusive discounts and offers on Packt books and eBooks.

https://www2.packtpub.com/books/subscription/packtlib

Do you need instant solutions to your IT questions? PacktLib is Packt's online digital book library. Here, you can search, access, and read Packt's entire library of books.

Why subscribe?

- Fully searchable across every book published by Packt
- Copy and paste, print, and bookmark content
- On demand and accessible via a web browser

Free access for Packt account holders

If you have an account with Packt at www.PacktPub.com, you can use this to access PacktLib today and view 9 entirely free books. Simply use your login credentials for immediate access.

Instant updates on new Packt books

Get notified! Find out when new books are published by following @PacktEnterprise on Twitter or the *Packt Enterprise* Facebook page.

Table of Contents

Preface

NetScaler is becoming more and more essential in many environments and is often crucial for many of the services it offers. *Mastering NetScaler VPX*™ is a book that covers many advanced topics, such as optimizing traffic, setting up redundant web services, and integrating with other Citrix products, as well as many best practices.

This book starts out with an easy introduction to the product, what it can offer, and how to do an initial setup on an on-premise deployment.

Later, it goes into some of the more advanced features, such as remote access against Citrix, different VPN features, and optimizing network services.

It also covers features of high availability such as GSLB, redirecting traffic using content switching, and different real-life scenarios and deployments.

What this book covers

Chapter 1, Configuring the Standard Features of NetScaler®, covers the basic setup of NetScaler, load balancing, and integration with XenDesktop.

Chapter 2, Using the Features of NetScaler® AppExpert, explains many of the different features found within AppExpert such as deployments of different templates, HTTP callout, rate limiting, rewrites, and responder policies.

Chapter 3, Integration with Citrix® Components, covers different integration possibilities with products such as Insight Center, CloudBridge, and Command Center.

Chapter 4, Traffic Management, illustrates many traffic management features, such as compression/caching, how to use content switching, and setting up GSLB.

Chapter 5, Tuning and Monitoring NetScaler® Performances, teaches you how to perform network optimization using TCP and SSL. This chapter also dives into the use of different tools for monitoring performance.

Chapter 6, Security Features and Troubleshooting, teaches you how to set up AAA, the use of security features such as HTTP DDoS, application firewalls, admin partitions, and lastly how you can troubleshoot using built-in tools and Wireshark.

Chapter 7, Real-World Deployment Scenarios, covers many real-life scenarios and shows how we can use NetScaler to set up a solution such as NetScaler Gateway for a small VDI environment, large web services spanning globally, and more.

What you need for this book

You can download a trial of the NetScaler virtual appliance from Citrix here: `https://secureportal.citrix.com/MyCitrix/login/EvalLand.aspx?download id=1857216&LandingFrom=1005`.

You should also have a virtual environment running any one of VMware, Citrix XenServer, or Hyper-V. If you do not have a virtual environment, you can test it on a client hypervisor.

For instance, if you are using Windows 8.1/10, you can use Client Hyper-V, which is an add-on that needs to be added from Programs and features under Control Panel.

Alternatively, you can use VMware Player (`https://my.vmware.com/web/vmware/ free#desktop_end_user_computing/vmware_player/6_0`).

Who this book is for

This book is intended for system administrators who work with either Citrix or networking and want to learn more advanced topics around Citrix NetScaler, such as integrating with other Citrix components or setting up advanced features such as GSLB and traffic optimization.

Conventions

In this book, you will find a number of styles of text that distinguish between different kinds of information. Here are some examples of these styles, and an explanation of their meaning.

Code words in text, database table names, folder names, filenames, file extensions, pathnames, dummy URLs, user input, and Twitter handles are shown as follows: "The expression will be SYS.HTTP_CALLOUT(NAMEOFTHECREATEDHTTPCALLOUT)."

A block of code is set as follows:

```
<resourcesWingConfigurations>
  <resourcesWingConfiguration name="Default" wingName="Default" />
</resourcesWingConfigurations>
```

When we wish to draw your attention to a particular part of a code block, the relevant lines or items are set in bold:

```
<optimalGatewayForFarmsCollection>
  <optimalGatewayForFarms enabledOnDirectAccess="{true | false}">
    <farms>
      <farm name="farmname" />
    </farms>
```

Any command-line input or output is written as follows:

```
show vpn icaconnection
show vpn stats
```

New terms and **important words** are shown in bold. Words that you see on the screen, in menus or dialog boxes for example, appear in the text like this: "Go to **AppExpert | HTTP Callouts** and click on **Add**."

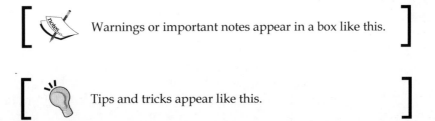

Warnings or important notes appear in a box like this.

Tips and tricks appear like this.

Reader feedback

Feedback from our readers is always welcome. Let us know what you think about this book—what you liked or may have disliked. Reader feedback is important for us to develop titles that you really get the most out of.

To send us general feedback, simply send an e-mail to feedback@packtpub.com, and mention the book title via the subject of your message.

If there is a topic that you have expertise in and you are interested in either writing or contributing to a book, see our author guide on www.packtpub.com/authors.

Customer support

Now that you are the proud owner of a Packt book, we have a number of things to help you to get the most from your purchase.

Downloading the example code

You can download the example code files for all Packt books you have purchased from your account at http://www.packtpub.com. If you purchased this book elsewhere, you can visit http://www.packtpub.com/support and register to have the files e-mailed directly to you.

Downloading the color images of this book

We also provide you a PDF file that has color images of the screenshots/diagrams used in this book. The color images will help you better understand the changes in the output. You can download this file from: https://www.packtpub.com/sites/default/files/downloads/B04217_1730EN_Graphics.pdf.

Errata

Although we have taken every care to ensure the accuracy of our content, mistakes do happen. If you find a mistake in one of our books—maybe a mistake in the text or the code—we would be grateful if you would report this to us. By doing so, you can save other readers from frustration and help us improve subsequent versions of this book. If you find any errata, please report them by visiting http://www.packtpub.com/submit-errata, selecting your book, clicking on the **errata submission form** link, and entering the details of your errata. Once your errata are verified, your submission will be accepted and the errata will be uploaded on our website, or added to any list of existing errata, under the Errata section of that title. Any existing errata can be viewed by selecting your title from http://www.packtpub.com/support.

Piracy

Piracy of copyright material on the Internet is an ongoing problem across all media. At Packt, we take the protection of our copyright and licenses very seriously. If you come across any illegal copies of our works, in any form, on the Internet, please provide us with the location address or website name immediately so that we can pursue a remedy.

Please contact us at copyright@packtpub.com with a link to the suspected pirated material.

We appreciate your help in protecting our authors, and our ability to bring you valuable content.

Questions

You can contact us at questions@packtpub.com if you are having a problem with any aspect of the book, and we will do our best to address it.

1

Configuring the Standard Features of NetScaler®

Welcome to the first chapter of this book. Throughout the course of this book, we will cover how to master Citrix NetScaler. This chapter will cover the most commonly used features of Citrix NetScaler.

Throughout this book, we will be focusing mostly on how to use the most common features of Citrix NetScaler. These features make Citrix NetScaler one of the best **Application Delivery Controller (ADC)**. The features will be available depending on the installed license. So, to sum it up, here's what we will cover throughout this chapter:

- Load balancing
- The NetScaler Gateway
- StoreFront integration
- Authentication

The basic features

During the installation, it's required to install the purchased license. Then, depending on the installed license, you will get the purchased functionality. The load balancing functionality is one of the most commonly used features in Citrix NetScaler. This is because of support from third-party vendors, which provide support and specific templates for particular services. These templates will be explained in the next chapter of this book. Besides load balancing, Citrix NetScaler is also capable of monitoring the backend that will be used to connect to, so you only connect to the backend machine if the system is healthy. This monitoring functionality is integrated in the load balancing feature. There are some monitoring configurations that are preconfigured. These can be adjusted if necessary. Also, uploading your own monitoring script is a possibility. Furthermore, the NetScaler Gateway is one of the commonly used features on Citrix NetScaler VPX. The NetScaler Gateway will be used to allow access to the Citrix XenApp/XenDesktop environment using an ICA proxy.

To configure Citrix NetScaler, it's necessary to understand the traffic flow in it. Citrix NetScaler uses a few IP addresses to operate:

- **NSIP**: This is the NetScaler IP address
- **MIP**: This is the Mapped IP address
- **SNIP**: This is the Subnet IP address
- **VIP**: This is the Virtual IP address

NSIP

The **NetScaler IP** address is the IP address for management purposes and is also used for authentication. So, it is used as the source IP against LDAP, RADIUS, WebForm, SAML, and so on. NSIP supports SSH, HTTP, and HTTPS by default. Disabling management is possible, if necessary.

MIP

The **Mapped IP** address is the IP address that is used for connectivity to the backend servers. This IP is still available but it's recommended to use the SNIP. The Subnet IP is preferred by Citrix because it allows you to have connectivity between different subnets. When receiving a packet, it replaces the source IP address with a MIP address before it sends the packet to the server. With the servers abstracted from the clients, the appliance manages connections more efficiently.

SNIP

The **Subnet IP** address is also an IP address that can be used for connectivity with the backend. A SNIP address is used in connection management and server monitoring. You can specify multiple SNIP addresses for each subnet. SNIP addresses can be bound to a VLAN. The latest firmware requires the use of SNIP during the installation wizard. Also, SNIP is used for DNS requires.

VIP

VIP is a **Virtual IP** address. This VIP address is used in every place where a client/server needs to communicate. The virtual IP is used in load balancing, AAA servers, access gateway virtual servers, and so on.

If you have multiple data centers that are geographically distributed, each data center can be identified by a unique GSLBIP.

Global Server Load Balancing Site IP Addresses (GSLBIPs) exist only on the NetScaler appliance.

IP set

An IP set is a set of IP addresses that are configured on the appliance as SNIP. An IP set is identified with a meaningful name that helps identify the usage of the IP addresses contained in it.

Net profile

A net profile (or network profile) contains an IP address or an IP set. A net profile can be bound to load balancing or content switching virtual servers, services, service groups, or monitors. During communication with physical servers or peers, the appliance uses the addresses specified in the profile as source IP addresses.

Load balancing

Load balancing is a feature that is implemented in most Citrix NetScaler environments. Load balancing allows you to load balance different backend servers with the same purpose, for example, a web shop. A large web shop requires more than one web server because of the heavy load from visiting users. With load balancing, Citrix NetScaler will load balance the traffic between the visiting servers and the several backend servers. Besides load balancing, Citrix NetScaler can also monitor the backend server if, for example, the web server responds with **HTTP Error code 200**.

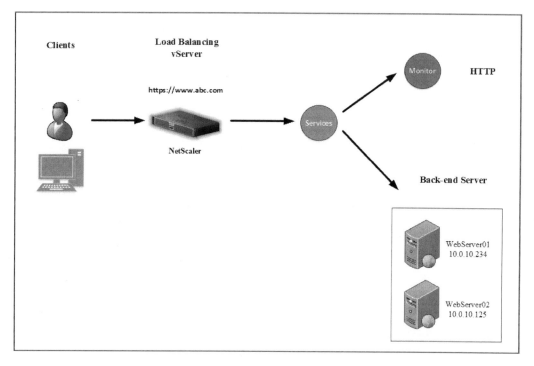

In order to configure the load balancing service in Citrix NetScaler, you need the following:

- **Servers**: This refers to the actually backend server that provides the information. In this case, it is an Apache web server.

  The IP address and server name are `10.0.10.234` for `webserver01` and `10.0.10.125` for `webserver02`.

- **Service/service group**: The service or service group is what provides the information to the user. A service is a particular server and a service group is a part of servers that provide the same information. Also, we bind a monitor to the service or service group. It checks the backend based on the configured monitor:
  - The service groups name is `LB_SG_WebServer`.
  - The members are `LB_SRV_WebServer01` and `LB_SRV_WebServer02`.
  - The used protocol is HTTP and the port is 80.
  - The configured monitor in this case is the HTTP monitor. This monitor checks of the `WebServer` responds with an HTTP 200 error.

- **Virtual server**: The load balancing virtual server is the actual virtual server that will be used to connect to. So, the user connects to this virtual server. Citrix NetScaler connects to the selected backend server, which is configured in the service / service group, based on the configured persistence or load balancing method:
  - **Virtual server name**: The virtual server name is `LB_VS_WebServer`. This virtual server name is only for your own information; choose a virtual server name that recognizes the service it's providing.
  - **VIP address**: This is the listing address of the load balancing service. In this example, it's DNS record is: `https://www.abc.com`. The DNS record was IP address: `192.168.12.87`.
  - **Protocol and port**: This is the responding protocol and port that the services respond to. Here, they are SSL and port 443.
  - **Services or service groups**: Select the proper service or service group responding with the load balancing service. This is the backend service that will be load-balanced. In the example, this would be service group `LB_SG_WebServer`.
  - **Load balancing method**: This option defines the load balancing method. There are a lot of options to select here. In this example, least bandwidth is used.
  - **Persistence**: This option defines the persistence. This persistence will be useful if you want the user to connect for a certain period of time to a particular backend server. In this case, it would be `COOKIEINSERT`.

Backup persistence

If the primary persistence can't be set, the backup persistence will be used, if configured. Use logical names for load balancing backend servers, services, service groups, and load balancing virtual servers. I prefer this so that it's always recognizable what the purpose of the item is. Some examples are LB_VS_ServiceName or LB_S_WebServer for a service, LB_SG_WebServers for service groups, and LB_SRV_ServerName for a backend server name.

So, in the default configuration, the user only has a web browser session with Citrix NetScaler, and Citrix NetScaler proxies the request to the backend server. Therefore, if the backend servers and Citrix NetScaler are in a demilitarized zone, the only firewall port from other networks should be the listen port of the load balancing virtual server.

When Citrix NetScaler is in the demilitarized zone, make sure that the MIP or SNIP has access to the backend. This is the source IP address that Citrix NetScaler uses to connect to the backend.

Active/active load balancing

With active/active, you load balance at least two backend machines with the same functionality. To configure active/active load balancing, it's necessary to create services or service groups for all backend servers that will be used for load balancing. While configuring active/active with different weights, I recommend that you use services instead of service groups, because you need to adjust the weight per service. Configuring active/active load balancing requires at least two services or service groups. Adjusting the weight while configuring the load balancing will change the percentage of traffic that will be sent to the backend server. Services or service groups with higher values can handle more requests; services or service groups with lower values can handle fewer requests. Assigning weights to services or service groups allows the Citrix NetScaler appliance to determine how much traffic each load-balanced server can handle and, therefore, balance the load more effectively.

In order to use active/active load balancing, it's necessary to configure the right persistence based on the requirement. In the following table, you can find all the persistence types available in Citrix NetScaler. This table also shows which persistence type will be available for a certain protocol:

Persistence type	HTTP	HTTPS	TCP	UDP/ IP	SSL_ Bridge	SSL_ TCP	RTSP	SIP_ UDP
SOURCEIP	YES	YES	YES	YES	YES	YES	NO	NO
COOKIEINSERT	YES	YES	NO	NO	NO	NO	NO	NO
SSLSESSION	NO	YES	NO	NO	YES	YES	NO	NO
URLPASSIVE	YES	YES	NO	NO	NO	NO	NO	NO
CUSTOMSERVERID	YES	YES	NO	NO	NO	NO	NO	NO
RULE	YES	YES	YES	NO	NO	YES	NO	NO
SRCIPDESTIP	YES	YES	YES	YES	YES	YES	NO	NO
DESTIP	YES	YES	YES	YES	YES	YES	NO	NO
CALLID	NO	NO	NO	NO	NO	NO	NO	YES
RTSPID	NO	NO	NO	NO	NO	NO	YES	NO

Setting a SOURCEIP persistence type for the load balancing vserver LB_VS_ WebServer through the command line can be done using this command:

```
set lb vserver LB_VS_WebServer -persistenceType SOURCEIP
```

In order to use the load balancing feature in a proper way, you should always select the right load balancing algorithms. Citrix NetScaler has a lot of built-in load balancing algorithms. These algorithms can be configured during the configuration of the load balancing virtual server and could be different from other load balancing virtual servers. The default load balancing algorithm is least connection. The different algorithms have been explained here:

- **Least connection**: This is the default algorithm. The backend service with the fewest active connections is used.

- **Round robin**: The first session will be connected to the service that is at the top of the list, the second session will be connected to the second service on the list, the third session will be connected to the third service, and so on. After the last service is connected, the connections will be started at the top of the list.

- **Least response time**: The service that has the fastest response will be used.

- **URL hash**: Citrix NetScaler creates a hash for every destination URL that is created for the first time. This hash will be cached. So, when the destination URL is contacted, Citrix NetScaler connects to the backend, connection is made to a URL for the first time, Citrix NetScaler creates a hash to that URL and caches it.

- **Domain hash**: Citrix NetScaler creates a hash for every first connecting domain. This hash will be cached. So, frequent connections to the same domain will contact the same service. The hash will be fetched from the HTTP header or from the URL.

- **Destination IP hash**: The destination IP hash will be created when a connection is made to an IP address for the first time. All traffic after the first connection will be forwarded to the same service.

- **Source IP hash**: This is same hash configuration as the destination IP; it's just that in this method the Source IP will be used.

- **Source destination IP hash**: Citrix NetScaler creates a hash based on the source and destination IP.

- **Call ID hash**: This creates a hash based on the call ID in the SIP header. This method makes sure that an SIP session is directed to the same backend server.

- **Source IP source port hash**: Citrix NetScaler creates a hash based on the source and source port.

- **Least bandwidth**: Least bandwidth will contact the service that uses the least bandwidth usage.

- **Least packets**: This method is based on the service with the fewest packets.

- **Custom load**: This method allows a user to create custom weights.

- **Token**: This method contacts the service based on a value from the configured expression.

- **LRTM**: This method contacts the service based on the least response time of the services.

So, after you have chosen the correct persistence type and algorithm, you can build the load balancing virtual server.

Active/passive load balancing

Citrix NetScaler also supports active/passive load balancing. This basically means that you have an active load balancing virtual server and another load balancing virtual server that will be used for passive load balancing. So, when all the services or service groups on the primary load balancing virtual server stop running, Citrix NetScaler will automatically will contact the backup load balancing virtual server. This functionality is widely used in environments with two different data centers, where one data center is passive. When the backend servers in the active load balancing virtual servers come back online, they will be the primary backend servers again instead the backend servers.

Load balancing StoreFront™

Citrix StoreFront is the replacement of Citrix Web Interface, which will end on June 30, 2018, if you have the software maintenance or subscription advantage. Otherwise, the end of life would be August 24, 2016. Besides, Citrix StoreFront allows you to work with the full-blown Citrix Receiver instead of only Receiver for Web. In order to load balance StoreFront, it is necessary that you install and configure Citrix StoreFront. To use the full-blown Citrix Receiver, it's necessary to configure Citrix StoreFront with an SSL certificate. This SSL certificate can be an internal certificate created by your own certificate authority, or it can be from a public certificate authority. When you are using your own certificate authority, for example, Microsoft, all clients will automatically trust the SSL certificate. Clients outside the Active Directory should install the root certificate to work with Citrix StoreFront and the full-blown Citrix Receiver.

In the following figure, you can find the most commonly used configuration for the load balancing of StoreFront:

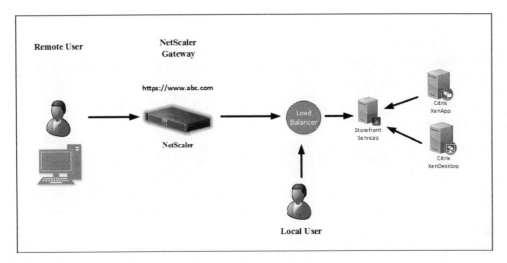

Citrix NetScaler is a good load balancer for the Citrix StoreFront environment. It contains a monitor for checking whether the StoreFront store is running and fully functional. This monitor is way better than the regular HTTPS monitor, because Citrix NetScaler also verifies that StoreFront is healthy. A lot of other vendors / load balancers can't do this because they don't have the value that is needed. Also, make sure you use service groups instead of services. Because the StoreFront monitor isn't the default monitor, the first step in load balancing Citrix StoreFront is to create the monitor.

Go to **Traffic Management | Load Balancing | Monitors**, and click on **Add**. Select **Type** as STOREFRONT from the list, and go to the **Special Parameters** tab. Fill in the **Store Name** field, as shown in the following screenshot. The store name can be found in the StoreFront console under the **Store** menu. Also add the monitor name and click on **Create**, as shown here:

The monitor can also be created using a command-line interface. The command required would be as follows:

```
add lb monitor storefront_ssl STOREFRONT -storename myStore
-storefrontacctservice YES -secure YES
```

Downloading the example code

You can download the example code files from your account at http://www.packtpub.com for all the Packt Publishing books you have purchased. If you purchased this book elsewhere, you can visit http://www.packtpub.com/support and register to have the files e-mailed directly to you.

The best way to create a load balancing environment is by starting from the bottom and going towards the top in the menu structure. In this way, you can create a decent name instead of the default names:

1. First, we need to add the backend servers that are running StoreFront to the server list.

2. The next step is to create a service group. This service group consists of the backend servers. Select the custom-made StoreFront monitor. This monitor will verify the StoreFront service even before the user connects to it. It's also possible to use the default monitor if you don't want any functionality checks. For troubleshooting or logging, it's very useful to have the client IP address. Because Citrix NetScaler operates as a load balancer, the source IP address to the backend servers will always be the SNIP. To have the client IP address as well, it's possible to insert the client IP into an HTTP header. This can be done while creating the service group. After you have added the backend servers, add the **Settings** menu on the right-hand side. Enable client IP and fill in the header box with *X-Forwarded-For*. Now, we are ready to create the load balancing virtual server.

3. Go to **Virtual Servers** and click on **Add**. Enter an IP address, a port, and a protocol. After this step, add the service group that you created in the preceding step. Depending on the configuration and the user access, we configure the proper protocol. If we also need support for the Citrix Receiver, we should use the SSL protocol because the Citrix Receiver requires a trusted communication. If this not necessary, the SSL certificate isn't required and we can use the HTTP protocol.

4. The regular deployments are SSL setups. After the members, protocol, IP address, and port are configured, we need to configure the persistence. This allows the user to stay connected to the same StoreFront server while working. The recommended settings are COOKIEINSERT and a timeout value from 0. The value 0 means that there is no expiry time. By configuring another timeout value, for example, 2 minutes, the user can connect to another StoreFront server. When this happens, the user needs to log in again, because there is no session available. As backup persistence, select SOURCEIP with the proper timeout. The timeout can't be zero and must be at least 2 minutes. When using the SSL protocol, we also need to add the certificate that is required for the load balancing virtual server.

5. When using SSL as the protocol, you should also consider disabling SSLv3 and enabling TLS 1.1 and TLS 1.2 on the load balancing virtual server. Since NetScaler 10.5 build 57.7 and higher, Citrix NetScaler supports TLS 1.1 and TLS 1.2 on the virtual appliance (VPX) as well. SSLv3 is an non-secure SSL protocol and should be disabled. This SSLv3 vulnerability is called POODLE (`https://en.wikipedia.org/wiki/POODLE`).

6. After creating the load balancing virtual server, the DNS record for the StoreFront base URL should be changed to the virtual IP from the load balancing virtual server.

When using Citrix StoreFront through SSL, configure the base URL and the load balancing virtual server, but bind the backend servers through HTTP. When you are using this deployment, Citrix NetScaler will be used as SSL offload functionality. However, please be aware that the credentials will be sent in plain text between Citrix NetScaler and the backend environment.

If you get the **Cannot complete your request** warning after connecting, there could be many reasons for it. For some explanations and fixes, refer to `http://support.citrix.com/article/CTX133904`.

Configuring authentication

Citrix NetScaler supports authentication for load balancing and access gateway purposes. The load balancing authentication is called the **authentication, authorization, and auditing (AAA)** functionality in Citrix NetScaler. By enabling the AAA feature on the load balancing virtual server, you can provide an extra security layer. The load balancing feature is a good solution for reverse proxy deployments. Enabling AAA on load balancing provides the extra security that you prefer to use for some services. While implementing AAA, it's also possible to add extra security (for example, two-factor authentication) to services that support only active directory authentication. So, Outlook Web Access for Microsoft Exchange can be configured with Active Directory and two-factor authentication. The NetScaler AAA features will redirect a load balancing virtual server to the NetScaler AAA virtual server. After authentication, the client will be sent back to the load balancing virtual server and will show the configured backend environment. So, the client connects to the load balancing virtual server for the Microsoft Exchange; NetScaler will redirect the client to the NetScaler AAA virtual servers. The client needs to log in. After successful authentication, NetScaler sends the client back to the load balancing virtual server.

Citrix NetScaler supports a lot of different methods of authentication. These methods can be used for NetScaler Gateway authentication or for load balancing virtual servers. The most common authentication methods will be described in the following sections.

> Authentication, Authorization, and Auditing (AAA) is available in the Enterprise and Platinum NetScaler license.

LDAP integration

LDAP integration is a commonly used method of authentication in deployments. Almost all companies are using LDAP authentication in some way. In order to use LDAP authentication, there are some prerequisites, as follows:

- A user account for "reading" the LDAP attributes
- The IP addresses from the LDAP servers
- How the user needs to log in (by username or e-mail address)
- Whether all users need access through LDAP authentication or any particular LDAP group
- Whether the LDAP server is responding with SSL or in PLAINTEXT

After you have the answers to these question, you can start building the configuration.

Go to **System** | **Authentication** | **LDAP** | **Servers**, and click on **Add**. Fill in the correct information based on the following explanation:

- **Name**: Select a decent name that responds to the LDAP server, for example, `Pol_Srv-LDAP-LDAPS1`.
- Select **Server Name** or **Server IP**. **Server Name** needs the FQDN, and **Server IP** needs the IP address from the LDAP server.
- **Security Type**: Select the available security type. It is preferable to use SSL because the credentials will not be sent in PLAINTEXT.
- **Server Type**: Select AD for Microsoft Active Directory or NDS if you're using Novell.

- **Base DN**: This box needs be filled in where Citrix NetScaler should look for users. If all the users are located in a particular organizational unit in Active Directory, it could be the **Base DN**. The less attributes needs be searched for the faster Citrix NetScaler will respond to the authentication questions. For example, a base DN for an organizational unit called Contoso Users in the `contoso.com` domain would look like `CN=Contoso Users,DC=CONTOSO,DC=COM`.

- **Administrator Bind DN**: This is the username for the AD or NDS that can be used for query the domain. This user doesn't require any specific security; domain users are okay. The username can be written in the `domain\username` or the `username@domain.suffix` method.

- **BindDN Password**: This will be the password from the configured administrator account, corresponding to the username that has filled in the **Administrator Bind DN** field.

- **Server Logon Name Attribute**: Commonly, this value contains the `sAMAccountName` or `UserPrincipalName` Active Directory / NDS attribute. Using the `UserPrincipalName` value allows you to log in with the e-mail address. Otherwise, the username is required to log in.

- **Search Filter**: This should be used if you'd like to allow access only for a particular Active Directory or NDS group. For example, you want to allow only the `AAA_Allow` group in the support `OU` to get the functionality to authenticate. The search filter would be `memberOf=CN=AAA_Allow,OU=support,DC=contoso,DC=com`. When a user is a member of this group, they will have access; otherwise, Citrix NetScaler will block the authentication. The source of this is `http://support.citrix.com/article/CTX111079`.

- **Group Attribute**: This will be used for group extraction. It's also possible to bind NetScaler Gateway policies to user groups. This will be explained later in the book. The default group attribute in the Active Directory /NDS is `memberOf`.

- **Sub Attribute Name**: This value is used to identify the subattribute name for group extraction.

- **SSO Name Attribute**: This attribute is used when **Single Sign On (SSO)** is configured. Depending on the backend, it should be `sAMAccountName` or `UserPrincipalName`.

 Use `SSL` as **Security Type** if possible. Besides, for security reasons, it always allows users to change their password remotely.

Name

vADC01

○ Server Name ● Server IP

Server Type*

AD ▼

IP Address*

192 . 168 . 20 . 205 ☐ IPv6

Time-out (seconds)

3

Security Type*

PLAINTEXT ▼

☑ Authentication

Port*

389

Connection Settings

Base DN (location of users)

CN=Contoso Users,DC=CONTOSO,D

☐ BindDN Password

Retrieve Attributes

Administrator Bind DN

admin@contoso.com

Other Settings

Server Logon Name Attribute

sAMAccountName ▼

Default Authentication Group

Search Filter

☑ User Required
☐ Referrals

Maximum Referral Level

Group Attribute

memberOf ▼

1

Referral DNS Lookup

Sub Attribute Name

cn ▼

A-REC ▼

☐ Validate LDAP Server Certificate

SSO Name Attribute

--<< New >>-- ▼

LDAP Host Name

sAMAccountName

After creating the LDAP servers, it's time to configure the LDAP Policies. These policies are necessary in order to bind it to a service. Depending on the configuration, there are many ways to configure it. With expressions, it is possible to, for example, allow access for specific client for a particular service. This will be done based on the *source IP* of the client and the *destination IP* for the particular service that you'd like to allow access to. The policy would be REQ.IP.SOURCEIP == 122.122.123.123 && REQ.IP.DESTIP == 192.168.100.14. In this example, the client with IP address 122.122.123.123 will be able to log in with the service 192.168.100.14.

It's also possible to add more than one LDAP authentication policy and bind them to the AAA or NetScaler Gateway authentication. This can be done by assigning priorities to the different policies. The LDAP policy with the lowest priority will be checked first to see whether the expression is matching. Otherwise, Citrix NetScaler will keep going down the list until it finds a match. If the policy matches but the server isn't responding within the configured timeout, Citrix NetScaler will automatically fill try the other expression.

Two-factor integration

Citrix NetScaler allows you to support two-factor authentication in many ways. The most commonly used way of two-factor authentication is by using the RADIUS protocol.

Most two-factor authentication providers support the RADIUS protocol because it's a standard protocol.

The RADIUS protocol uses a few codes to indicate the authentication step, as follows:

Code	Assignment
1	Access-Request
2	Access-Accept
3	Access-Reject
4	Accounting-Request
5	Accounting-Response
11	Access-Challenge

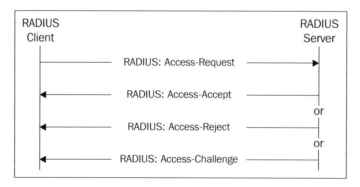

Depending on what the RADIUS server sends back, Citrix NetScaler will allow or deny the access to log in.

Go to **System | Authentication | RADIUS | Servers**, and click on **Add**. Fill in the correct information based on the following explanation:

- **Name**: Select a decent name that responds to the RADIUS server, for example, `Pol_Srv-RADIUS-RADIUSS1`.

- Select **Server Name** or **Server IP**. **Server Name** needs the FQDN, and **Server IP** needs the IP address from the RADIUS server.

- **Port**: This is the RADIUS port.

- **Time-out (seconds)**: This is the time that the RADIUS server has to respond to Citrix NetScaler.

- **Secret Key**: On the RADIUS server, a RADIUS client should also be created. This RADIUS client configuration requires a shared key. This key will be created during the configuration at the RADIUS server. The secret key needs to be filled in this box.

- **NAS ID**: By default, Citrix NetScaler will send the hostname from the device. With the NAS ID, Citrix NetScaler will send the identifier configured in this box.

- **Group Vendor Identifier**: This is the RADIUS vendor ID attribute. It is used for RADIUS group extraction.

- **Group Prefix**: This is the RADIUS group's prefix string. This group prefix precedes the group names within a RADIUS attribute for RADIUS group extraction.

- **Group Attribute Type**: This is the attribute number that contains the group information.

- **Group Separator**: This is the group separator string that delimits group names within a RADIUS attribute for RADIUS group extraction.

- **IP Address Vendor Identifier**: This is the vendor ID of the Intranet IP attribute in the RADIUS response. The default value of 0 indicates that the attribute is not vendor encoded.

- **IP Address Attribute Type**: This is the remote IP address attribute type in a RADIUS response.

- **Password Vendor Identifier**: This is the vendor ID of the attribute in the RADIUS response. It is used to extract the user's password.

- **Password Attribute Type**: This is the vendor-specific password attribute type in a RADIUS response.

- **Password Encoding**: This is the encoding type for passwords in the RADIUS packets that the NetScaler appliance sends to the RADIUS server. Citrix NetScaler supports PAP, CHAP, MS-CHAPv1, and MS-CHAPv2. MS-CHAPv2 is the most secure method.

- **Accounting**: This allows Citrix NetScaler to support accounting. It can be ON or OFF.

- **Default Authentication Group**: This is the default group that is chosen when the authentication succeeds in addition to extracted groups.

 When using RADIUS authentication, it's necessary to create a RADIUS client on the RADIUS server. This RADIUS client will be Citrix NetScaler. The RADIUS client's IP address would be the NetScaler IP (NSIP).

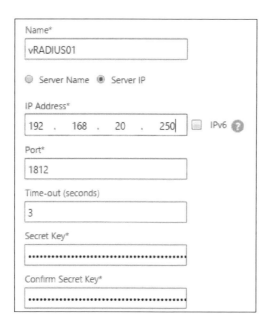

After creating the RADIUS servers, it's time to configure the RADIUS Policies. These policies are necessary for binding it to services.

It's also possible to add more than one RADIUS authentication policy and bind them to the AAA or NetScaler Gateway authentication. This can be done by assigning priorities to the different policies. The way of configuring is the same as that for binding the LDAP authentication policy.

Citrix wrote an article on how to configure Citrix NetScaler with Microsoft NPS. Microsoft NPS is the RADIUS server from Microsoft. A lot of third-party vendors have written plugins for NPS server. An article that can be used is `http://support.citrix.com/article/CTX126691`.

Configuring NetScaler® AAA

To allow extra security with authentication on the load balancing features, we should use the Citrix NetScaler AAA feature. With the following steps, we can secure a load balancing virtual server with two-factor authentication based on Web Form authentication:

1. Go to **Security** | **AAA - Application Traffic** | **Policies** | **Sessions** | **Session Profiles**, and click on **Add**.

   Fill in the correct information based on the following explanation:

   ○ **Name**: Select a decent name that responds to the AAA Session Profile, for example, AAA-Pro-Session.

   ○ **Session Time-out (mins)**: The timeout before Citrix NetScaler kills the session.

   ○ **Default Authorization Action**: This can be ALLOW or DENY. Select ALLOW.

   ○ **Single Sign-on to Web Applications**: Enable this if you want SSON in the backend.

   ○ **Credential Index**: Use the primary or secondary authentication policy for SSON.

   ○ **Single Sign-on Domain**: This will be the internal domain name from the AD or NDS.

   ○ **HTTPOnly Cookie**: Allow only an HTTP session cookie, in which case the cookie cannot be accessed by scripts.

   ○ **Enable Persistent Cookie**: You can enable or disable persistent SSO cookies for the **traffic management (TM)** session. A persistent cookie remains on the user device and is sent with each HTTP request.

   ○ **Persistent Cookie Validity**: This is an integer specifying the number of minutes for which the persistent cookie remains valid.

- ○ **KCD Account**: Kerberos constrains the delegation account name when using Kerberos authentication.
- ○ **Home Page**: This is the web address of the home page that a user is displayed when the authentication vserver is bookmarked and used to log in.

2. Go to **Security | AAA - Application Traffic | Policies | Sessions | Session Policies**, and click on **Add**:

- ○ **Name**: Select a decent name that responds to the AAA Session Policy, for example, `AAA-Pol-Session`.
- ○ **Request Profile**: Select the profile created in step 1.
- ○ **Expression**: You can bind an expression. In this case, we use `ns_true`.

3. Go to **Security | AAA - Application Traffic | Virtual Servers**, and click on **Add**. Fill in the correct information based on this explanation:

- ○ **Name**: Again, select a decent name that responds to the AAA virtual server, for example, `AAA-Srv-TwoFactor`.
- ○ **IP Address Type**: Select IP address, or non addressable if you want to use the content switching method.
- ○ **Port**: This is the AAA virtual server port. The default is `443`.
- ○ **Authentication Domain**: This would be the domain from the public site, for example, `contoso.com`.

4. Bind the certificate.
5. Bind the session policy created in step 2.
6. Bind the **Basic Authentication Policies**, Add `LDAP` as **Primary**, and add the `RADIUS` as **Secondary**. Click on **Continue**.
7. Go to **Security | AAA - Application Traffic | Authentication Profile**, and click on **Add**. Fill in the correct information based on the explanations given here:

- ○ **Name**: Select a decent name that responds to the AAA virtual server, for example, `AAA-AuthPol-TwoFactor`
- ○ **Authentication Host**: This would be the FQDN where the NetScaler AAA virtual server would respond to, for example, `twofactor.contoso.com`.
- ○ **Choose Authentication Virtual Server Type**: Choose `Authentication Virtual Server`

- ○ **Authentication Virtual Server**: Select the `Authentication Virtual Server` created in step 3

- ○ **Authentication Domain**: This would be the domain from the public site, for example, `contoso.com`

- ○ **Authentication Level**: Fill in the value as 1 if you are using one authentication method, and 2 if you are using two-factor authentication

8. Open the **Load Balancing Virtual Server** that you want to protect. Add the **Authentication** from the right-hand side of the page.

9. Select **Form Based Authentication** or **401 Based Authentication**. In this case, we're using **Form Based Authentication**. This is because we wish to use two-factor authentication:

10. **Authentication FQDN**: This is the FQDN from the NetScaler AAA virtual server, for example, `twofactor.contoso.com`.

- ○ **Choose Authentication Virtual Server Type**: Choose `Authentication Virtual Server`

- ○ **Authentication Virtual Server**: Select the `Authentication Virtual Server` created in step 3

- ○ **Authentication Profile**: Select the `Authentication Policy` created in step 7

11. Now your **Load Balancing Virtual Server** is protected with the NetScaler AAA security:

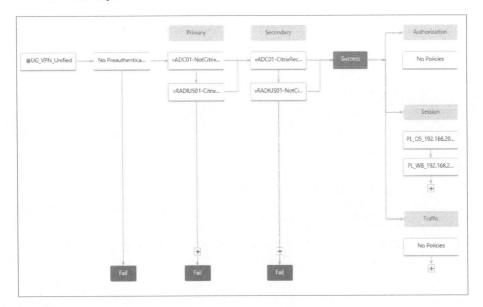

Citrix Receiver™ authentication

If you want to use the Citrix Receiver functionality and Receiver for Web with the NetScaler Gateway environment as well, some changes should be made to the LDAP and RADIUS policies. You should make some adjustments to the expressions.

When a user contacts the NetScaler Gateway through the web browser, they will see three fields that need to be filled in.

The first box requires the username, the second requires the password, and the third requires the RADIUS code. This means that the LDAP authentication is primary and RADIUS is the secondary authentication. You can see this in the following screenshot:

When the user connects with Citrix Receiver, the authentication is different because Citrix Receiver verifies the RADIUS authentication as primary and the LDAP authentication as secondary.

In order to arrange this, we should create two different LDAP and RADIUS policies. The LDAP policies could bind to the same LDAP server. The RADIUS policies could be bind to the same RADIUS server as well.

Follow these steps to arrange authentication through Citrix Receiver when using two-factor authentication:

1. Create two LDAP policies:

    ◦ **Policy 1**:

    Name: `CitrixReceiver-DC1` (where `DC1` is the domain controller name)

    Expression: `REQ.HTTP.HEADER User-Agent CONTAINS CitrixReceiver`

    Server: `DC1`

    ° **Policy 2**:

    Name: `NonCitrixReceiver-DC1` (where `DC1` is the domain controller name)

    Expression: `REQ.HTTP.HEADER User-Agent NOTCONTAINS CitrixReceiver`

    Server: `DC1`

2. Create two RADIUS policies:

    ° **Policy 1**:

    Name: `CitrixReceiver-RADIUS1` (where `RADIUS1` is the RADIUS server)

    Expression: `REQ.HTTP.HEADER User-Agent CONTAINS CitrixReceiver`

    Server: `RADIUS1`

    Policy 2:

    Name: `NonCitrixReceiver-RADIUS1` (where `RADIUS1` is the RADIUS server)

    Expression: `REQ.HTTP.HEADER User-Agent NOTCONTAINS CitrixReceiver`

    Server: `RADIUS1`

3. Bind the `NonCitrixReceiver-DC1` LDAP policy and the `CitrixReceiver-RADIUS1` RADIUS policy as the primary authentication.

4. Bind the `CitrixReceiver-DC1` LDAP policy and the `NonCitrixReceiver-RADIUS1` RADIUS policy as the secondary authentication.

When the user connects through Citrix Receiver, the authentication flow would first be `CitrixReceiver-RADIUS1` as primary and `CitrixReceiver-DC1` as secondary, because Citrix Receiver contains the `User-Agent` header with the `CitrixReceiver` value. All other non-Citrix Receiver users will authenticate with `NonCitrixReceiver-DC1` as primary authentication and `NonCitrixReceiver-RADIUS1` as secondary authentication.

Troubleshooting

For troubleshooting authentication, Citrix NetScaler provides a built-in tool that can be run from the CLI. Connect to the CLI with an SSH tool (PuTTY, for example). After logging in, type `shell` and then jump to the `tmp` location using `cd /tmp`. Run the following command after switching to the `tmp` location:

```
cat aaaa.debug
```

This built-in tool will give us information about what's going wrong during authentication.

Besides the built-in tool, Citrix also provides troubleshoot logging according to authentication in the GUI since NetScaler firmware release 11. So, if you are using Citrix NetScaler 11, troubleshooting through CLI isn't necessary.

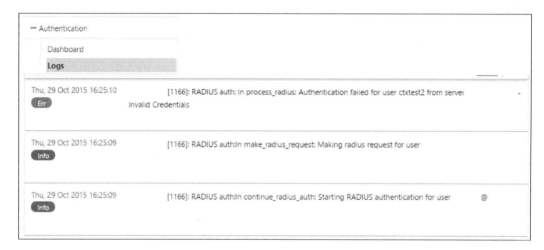

NetScaler Gateway™

NetScaler Gateway is the new name for the Citrix Access Gateway. Citrix changed the name because the access gateway is a feature from NetScaler. The NetScaler Gateway can be used for ICA Proxy. Also, Citrix released the functionality of using the NetScaler as an RDP Proxy in NetScaler 11. The RDP Proxy is available with Enterprise and Platinum licensing. Also, the NetScaler Gateway supports the secure browser-only access (CVPN) functionality. The NetScaler Gateway will be installed most of the time in the demilitarized zone, because this VIP will be used through the Internet.

Session policies

Session policies will be used after the authentication, if successful. Based on the configuration in the session policy, the connected user will get to see the resources, for example, the StoreFront web page or a connection through VPN. A session policy always contains two parts: the session policy and the session profile. The session profile indicates what NetScaler needs to show. The session policy is the policy that needs to match to display what is configured in the session profile.

The session profile contains a lot of options and can handle multiple configurations. So, based on screenshots, we will explain the options.

> The Citrix NetScaler Gateway session settings can be configured on the global level and based on session policies. When settings are made on the global level, all configured settings will be set for all available NetScaler Gateway virtual servers. Using session policies, we can define settings that are different for every available NetScaler Gateway virtual server. So, while creating a session profile / session policy, make sure that the **Override Global** setting is selected to make adjustments for this particular setting.

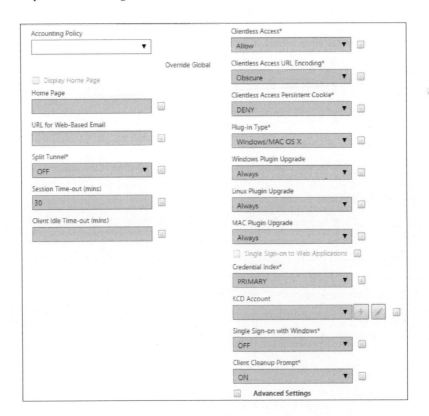

The **Network Configuration** pane will not be used most of the time, so in this case, we will skip this part. Under the **Client Experience** pane, we have multiple settings that we can define. All of these settings will be explained next. Some of these settings are necessary for ICA Proxy, and some of them are used for VPN. The available settings under the **Client Experience** pane are as follows:

- **Home Page**: This is used while connecting through a VPN setting. Configuring this setting will show the home page that is entered here.

- **URL for Web-Based Email**: This setting is for users to log in to web-based e-mail solutions, for example, OWA.

- **Split Tunnel**: With this setting, we can define whether all client traffic or only the traffic meant for destined servers in the network should go through the gateway in a VPN connection.

- **Session Time-out (mins)**: This configures how long Citrix NetScaler keeps the session active when there is no network traffic. This applies to ICA Proxy and VPN as well. Default time-out is 30 minutes.

- **Client Idle Time-out (mins)**: This defines how long NetScaler waits before it disconnects the session when there is no user activity. This only applies to NetScaler Gateway plugins.

- **Clientless Access**: This defines whether the SSL-based VPN should be enabled or disabled.

- **Clientless Access URL Encoding**: This setting allows us to change the visibility of the URL from internal web applications. The options are obscured, encrypted, or in clear text.

- **Clientless Access Persistent Cookie**: This is needed for access to certain features when using clientless VPN.

- **Plug-in Type**: This setting defines the kind of plugin offered to the user—whether it is Windows/Mac-based or Java-based. It is used for VPN connections.

- **Single Sign-on to Web Applications**: This setting allows NetScaler Gateway to perform Single Sign-on to the configured web interface address.

- **Credential Index**: This setting allows us to choose which authentication credentials are to be forwarded to the web application. Here, we can choose from the primary or the secondary authentication set.

- **Single Sign-on with Windows**: This setting allows the NetScaler Gateway plug-in to authenticate using the Windows credentials.

- **Client Cleanup Prompt**: This is a prompt for client-side cache cleanup when a client-initiated session closes. This feature is not available for mobile devices.

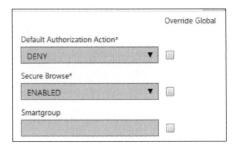

In the **Security** pane, all that we need to do is make sure that the **Default Authorization Action** option is set to Allow. This ensures that the users are actually allowed to log in and access the resources. The **Secure Browse** option will be used in combination with Citrix XenMobile only. This option allows users to connect through NetScaler Gateway to network resources from iOS and Android mobile devices with Citrix Receiver. Users do not need to establish a full VPN tunnel to access the resources in the secure network. The **Smartgroup** option will be used for **Endpoint Analysis (EPA)**. This option contains the group in which the user is placed when the session policy associated with this session action succeeds. The VPN session policy will do the post-auth EPA check, and if the check succeeds, the user will be placed in the group specified with smartgroup.

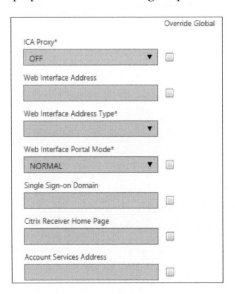

Next, we have the **Published Applications** pane. This is where we enter the information needed to access our Citrix environment. The following are the settings:

- **ICA Proxy**: This setting allows us to define whether the virtual server should be used as ICA Proxy through SSL or not.

- **Web Interface Address**: This box contains the URL to the Citrix Web Interface or the Citrix StoreFront Receiver for Web URL.

- **Web Interface Portal Mode**: This setting allows you to define whether the configured web interface should appear with full graphical experience or in compact view.

- **Single Sign-on Domain**: This setting defines the AD or NDS domain that will be used for single sign-on.

- **Citrix Receiver Homepage**: This setting will be used for a client's connection to a Citrix Receiver that doesn't support Citrix StoreFront. This box contains another URL for the client to connect to.

- **Account Services Address**: This setting will be used for e-mail-based account discovery for Citrix Receiver. The URL must be in the form of `https://<StoreFront/AppController URL>/Citrix/Roaming/Accounts`. This requires that the DNS be properly configured because there should be some SRV DNS records created, and it requires a wildcard certificate, or a certificate that contains `discoverReceiver.domain` in the **Subject** or **Subject Alternative Name** entry. For more information, refer to `https://www.citrix.com/blogs/2013/04/01/configuring-email-based-account-discovery-for-citrix-receiver/`

After creating the session profiles, there should also be a session policy created in order to bind this to a NetScaler Gateway virtual server. As we want all users to be bound to this policy, we use the `ns_true` general expression, as shown in the following screenshot:

After the session policies have been created, the NetScaler Gateway virtual server can be created. Follow these steps to create a NetScaler Gateway virtual server based:

1. Go to **NetScaler Gateway | Virtual Server**, and click on **Add**.

   Fill in the correct information based on the following explanation:

   - ° **Name**: Select a decent name that responds to the NetScaler Gateway virtual server, for example, VS_CAG_Server1.
   - ° **IP Address Type**: Select the corresponding IP address.
   - ° **Port**: Select the proper port. The default is 443.
   - ° Select **ICA Only** if you're using only ICA traffic. Otherwise leave this unselected. If you are not using the **ICA Only** mode, it's necessary to have the Citrix Universal Gateway license installed on Citrix NetScaler.

2. Bind the proper certificate.

3. Configure the proper authentication methods.

4. Then bind the session policies.

5. Configure the published application.

After these steps, we will have a fully configured NetScaler Gateway function on Citrix NetScaler. Citrix StoreFront needs to be configured as well in order to user pass-through authentication through the NetScaler Gateway.

> Disable SSLv3 and enable TLS1.1 and TLS1.2 for security purposes. Also make sure that the RC4 SSL ciphers are removed. RC4 and SSLv3 are security leaks and need to be disabled right away.
>
> If we wish to use the HTML5 Citrix Receiver, it's necessary to enable the Enable WebSocket connections in the HTTP profile in Citrix NetScaler.

Integration StoreFront™

To use Citrix StoreFront with the NetScaler Gateway, we need to create session policies on the NetScaler Gateway and configure Citrix StoreFront for pass-through authentication through it. We will start by creating session profiles / session policies on the NetScaler Gateway.

Citrix StoreFront always wants to use pass-through for Citrix NetScaler, even when the authentication method is disabled. To disable pass-through authentication in Citrix StoreFront, we need to disable **requireTokenConsistency** in `inetpub\` `wwwroot\<storename>\web.config`.

Citrix Receiver™

One of the benefits of the Citrix Receiver configuration with Citrix StoreFront is their integration with each other. The Citrix Receiver automatically detects whether the user is an internal user or an external user. When it detects an external connection, it will connect through the NetScaler Gateway; otherwise, it will use the Citrix StoreFront authentication. This detecting will be done by the configured beacons in the Citrix StoreFront configuration. During the configuration of the Citrix Receiver, the beacons will be configured.

Now it's time to configure the Citrix Receiver session policy and profile in the NetScaler Gateway.

Create a new session policy and go to the **Client experience** pane. Change **Clientless Access** to `Allow`, change the **Plug-in Type** to `Java`, and enable **Single Sign-on** to `Web Applications`. If we are using two-factor authentication, we also need to change **Credential Index** to `Secondary`. As explained before, the Citrix Receiver authenticates in a different way; in order to support single sign-on, it's necessary to use the LDAP authentication for single sign-on authentication.

Go to the **Published Application** pane. Switch **ICA Proxy** to `ON`. **Web Interface Address** should be `StoreFront URL`. Change **Web Interface Address Type** to `IPv4`, change **Single Sign-on Domain** to the `AD` or `NDS` domain name, and at least fill in **Account Services Address** with the `https://<StoreFront/Citrix/Roaming/` `Accounts` value.

After these settings, the session profile is done. Now it's time to create the session policy. The expression would be `REQ.HTTP.HEADER User-Agent CONTAINS` `CitrixReceiver` in this case.

The session policy is explained in this chapter, under the *NetScaler Gateway* section, *Session policies*.

Receiver for Web

Create a new session policy and go to the **Client experience** pane. Change **Clientless Access** to ON and enable **Single Sign-on** to Web Applications.

Go to the **Published Application** pane. Switch **ICA Proxy** to ON. **Web Interface Address** should be StoreFront Receiver For Web URL. Change **Web Interface Address Type** to IPv4, and then change **Single Sign-on Domain** to the AD or NDS domain name.

After these settings, the session profile is done. Now it's time to create the session policy. The expression would be REQ.HTTP.HEADER User-Agent NOTCONTAINS CitrixReceiver in this case.

Citrix® StoreFront™

First, we need to add a gateway to StoreFront. This can be done from the GUI by navigating to **StoreFront Administration Console | NetScaler Gateways**. On the right-hand side here, click on **Add NetScaler Gateway Appliance** and then add the information as shown in the following screenshot:

- **Display name**: Use NetScaler Gateway.

- **NetScaler Gateway URL**: Fill in the box with the proper NetScaler Gateway URL. Citrix StoreFront requires this URL to verify that this configuration matches the NetScaler Gateway URL.

- **Subnet IP address**: This box is optional and should be left empty if possible. It can be filled in if we are using more than one Citrix NetScaler Gateway on one Citrix NetScaler pointing to the same Citrix StoreFront environment.

- **Logon type**: Select the proper log-on type. Use Domain and security token if you are using two-factor authentication and Domain only if you are using single-factor authentication.

- **Callback URL**: The Callback URL field needs to point to the VIP address of NetScaler Gateway. This is needed so that Citrix StoreFront can send the validation back to the NetScaler Gateway authentication service.

Now, for the final part in Citrix StoreFront. The configured NetScaler Gateway appliance needs to be connected to a particular Citrix StoreFront store for external authentication. Navigate to the **Store** menu and click on the right-hand side of the console, on the **Enable Remote Access** button. Now, we have to specify whether the store will be available for external usage. The following are the settings:

- **None**: This means that the store can't be used for external users.

- **No VPN Tunnel**: This option makes the store available through Citrix NetScaler Gateway without the NetScaler Gateway plugin.

- **Full VPN Tunnel**: This option makes the store available through an SSL VPN only. It requires the NetScaler Gateway plugin.

As long as we don't need the VPN tunnel support, we select **NO VPN Tunnel**. We mark the Citrix NetScaler appliance that we added earlier. Propagate the changes to the other Citrix StoreFront if you have more than one Citrix StoreFront server.

Group policies

Citrix NetScaler provides support to bind sessions, traffic, authorization, bookmarks, Intranet IP addresses, and Intranet applications based on groups. When the authentication policies are configured correctly, it's possible to extract Active Directory groups from the connecting users. If we want to bind an authorization policy to an Active Directory, it's necessary to add the group in the NetScaler Gateway. This can be done in **AAA Groups** in the **User Administration** menu under the **NetScaler Gateway** pane. Please be aware that this group name is exactly the same as the group name in Active Directory; it's key sensitive.

SmartAccess filters

Citrix NetScaler 11 supports SmartAccess in NetScaler itself. Citrix calls this feature SmartAccess 2.0. These policies can be bound to the NetScaler Gateway virtual servers and allow you to disable or enable features. These features are called **ICA Policies** in NetScaler 11.

Summary

This chapter described the basic features of the NetScaler ADC, the different load balancing functionalities, the NetScaler AAA feature, the NetScaler Gateway, and how to configure the Citrix NetScaler Gateway with Citrix StoreFront.

It's not possible to explain all the possible deployments from the NetScaler Gateway from the load balancing features in just one chapter. There are a lot of other deployments available. For example, it's possible to use the NetScaler Gateway as an RDP gateway.

 For more information about the possible deployments, see the Citrix documentation. The URL is `http://docs.citrix.com/en-us/netscaler-gateway/11/deploy-xenmobile.html`.

In the next chapter, we will explain the use of the Citrix NetScaler AppExpert features.

2
Using the Features of NetScaler® AppExpert

AppExpert's features are one of the most used features available in Citrix NetScaler. Most of AppExpert's features are included in the Citrix NetScaler Standard licensing. With AppExpert's features, we're able to make adjustments too, for example, HTTP headers and prevent services for **Denial-of-Service** (**DOS**) attacks. Citrix NetScaler offers seamless compatibility with your infrastructure through configuration templates for key Microsoft applications and built-in system center integration. Setup wizards and AppExpert templates make integrating and configuring NetScaler with Microsoft technologies easy. These extensible templates provide preconfigured policies for advanced optimizations, such as caching and compression. They even replicate the exact configurations that your business needs by modifying existing templates.

NetScaler has been validated to enhance user experience with these applications, whether they are accessed locally or across the globe. NetScaler provides compression, caching, load balancing, and SSL acceleration to improve SharePoint response times by over 80 percent. With a 150-fold reduction in client-to-server connections, data center expenses are dramatically reduced. All the available AppExpert features will be explained in this chapter.

AppExpert applications and templates

Citrix provides templates that can be downloaded from their website. These templates simplify deployment of services. They include load balancing rules, compression, redirecting, caching rules, and so on. The template can be found at http://www.citrix.com/static/appexpert/appexpert-template.html.

Note that AppExpert templates are based on the default settings from Citrix and require adjustments before they can be used in a production environment. The AppExpert Templates feature is available under the **AppExpert** menu. After downloading the template from the URL mentioned previously, we can import the template and the deployment file. This can be done by clicking on **Import Template** under the **Applications** pane in the **AppExpert** menu:

1. Fill in **Application Name**. In this case, we're implementing the Microsoft Exchange template, so the name should be something like MicrosoftExchange.

2. Upload the template file and, if necessary, the deployment file.

3. Click on **Continue**, as shown here:

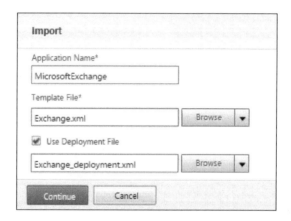

 Application Name can contain a space. The name must begin with an alphanumeric character or underscore and can contain only alphanumerics, _, #, ., :, @, =, or, -.

In this case, the template file for Microsoft Exchange contains information about rewrite, load balancing settings (persistence and the load balancing method), and so on.

The deployment file contains information about the content switching listeners and the Microsoft Exchange server itself.

If you upload the deployment file, make sure that the IP address matches that of your environment. Changing the XML file before uploading the file will result in a configuration that is production ready in this case.

After you have implemented **AppExpert Template**, the configuration in Citrix NetScaler looks likes what is shown in the following diagram:

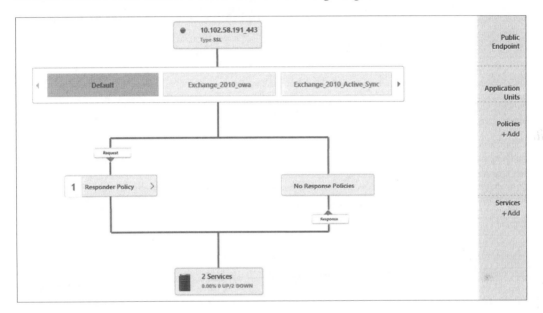

After importing the template, verification is important.

The **graphical user interface (GUI)** includes icons that indicate the states of the entities in the AppExpert application. These icons are displayed for applications and application units, and are based on the health checks that the NetScaler appliance performs periodically on services and entities.

You must ensure that the icons for each application and its application units are green at all times. If the icon that is displayed for an application is not green, verify that you have configured the public endpoints correctly. If the icon that is displayed for an application unit is not green, verify that the services are configured correctly. However, note that a green indicator does not mean that the state of all associated entities is UP. It only means that the application has sufficient resources (endpoints and services) to serve client requests.

HTTP Callouts

The HTTP Callouts option will be used for configured types of requests, or when criteria are met during policy evaluation. When the criteria matches the type of request, you might want to stall the policy evaluation briefly, retrieve information from a server, and then perform an action depending on the retrieved information. Another option could be that you want to update a database or the content hosted on a web server based on the requests.

An HTTP Callout is an HTTP or HTTPS request that Citrix NetScaler generates and sends to an external resource when the criteria matches during policy evaluation. The information can be analyzed by default syntax policy expressions.

You can use HTTP Callouts to obtain information from external applications. The Callout policy sends an HTTP request to an external application. An agent that you deploy in front of the application formats the request for the application.

The HTTP Callout can be configured for HTTP or HTTPS content switching, TCP content switching, rewrites, responders, and token-based load balancing methods.

To perform the HTTP Callout function, we must set up an application on the server that will be used to send the HTTP Callout. This server/application will called the HTTP Callout agent and must respond with the required information. The HTTP Callout agent can be a web server that serves the data for which Citrix NetScaler sends the callout. We have to make sure that the format of the response to an HTTP Callout doesn't change from one invocation to another.

After we have set up the HTTP Callout agent, we can configure the HTTP Callout on Citrix NetScaler. In order to use the HTTP Callout, we need to include the Callout in a default syntax policy and bind the policy to the bind point which we want the policy to be evaluated.

How HTTP Callout works

When receiving a request from the client, Citrix NetScaler evaluates the request against the configured policies bounded to various bind points. During the evaluation from the policies, Citrix NetScaler will stall the policy evaluation when the HTTP Callout expression is being used. The expression will be SYS.HTTP_CALLOUT(name). When Citrix NetScaler receives the response, it will either perform an action or jump to the next policy depending on the evaluation of the response from the HTTP Callout agent as FALSE or TRUE.

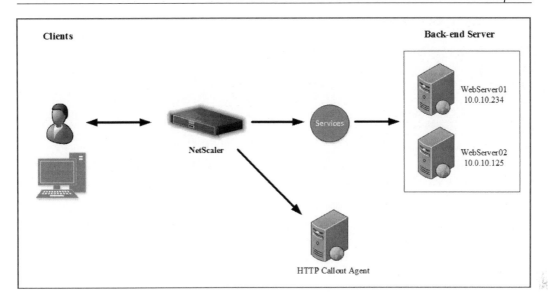

The preceding figure demonstrates the working of an HTTP Callout request based on a bound responder policy on NetScaler load balancing. The NetScaler load balancing virtual server has an HTTP Callout configured to allow only specific incoming requests. When Citrix NetScaler receives a request from a client or device that's contacting the NetScaler load balancing virtual server, the appliance will generate the HTTP Callout request and send it to the configured HTTP Callout agent. The HTTP Callout agent will receive the request and verify the requested URL. If the requested URL matches the allowed expression, the HTTP Callout agent will forward the requested response to the configured services. If the requested URL doesn't match, Citrix NetScaler will reset the client connection.

Configuring HTTP Callout

To work with the HTTP Callout functionality, we have to start by enabling the responder feature. The responder policy will also be explained in this chapter, but for HTTP Callout, we won't provide too much information about the working of the responder feature.

Go to **AppExpert | HTTP Callouts** and click on **Add**. Fill in the correct information based on the following explanation:

- **Name**: This will be the name where the HTTP Callout will be named to.
- **Comment**: Here, we can add a comment if necessary.

- **Server to receive callout request**: Select the corresponding virtual server or enter the IP address that will be used as the HTTP Callout agent in this HTTP Callout configuration.

- **Request Type**: Select the proper request type. This can be `Attribute-based` or `Expression-based`. With `Attribute-based`, it's possible to use an attribute in the URL for example. With `Expression-based`, we can only use expressions based on the functionalities in Citrix NetScaler, for example, `CLIENT.IP.SRC`.

- **Method**: This option is available only when `Attribute-based` is selected under **Request Type**. Select the corresponding method. It can be `GET` or `POST`.

- **Host Expression**: This option is available only when you select `Attribute-based` under **Request Type**. It contains the string expression for configuring the host header. It can also contain a value such as the IP address of the backend machine or the host request header.

- **URL Stem Expression**: This option is available only when you select `Attribute-based` under **Request Type**. In this expression, the generating URL needs to be filled in. So, the request URL should be entered here, which will be sent to the HTTP Callout server.

- **Body Expression**: Again, this option is only available when `Attribute-based` is selected. It can contain an advanced string expression for generating the body of the request.

- **Headers**: This option is available only when you select `Attribute-based` under **Request Type**. It contains information for identifying that it's about a Callout request. Normally, the name would be `Request` and **Value-expression** would be `Callout Request`.

- **Parameters**: This option too is available only when you select `Attribute-based` under **Request Type**. The parameter sends the requested information to the backend. For example, consider the parameter name `ClientIP` with **Value-expression** as `CLIENT.IP.SRC`. The `ClientIP` parameter can request by the HTTP Callout agent to request the source IP from the client.

- **Full Expression**: This option is available only when you select `Expression-based` under **Request Type**. It needs the exact HTTP request in the form of an expression, which Citrix NetScaler sends to the HTTP Callout agent.

- **Scheme**: Select `HTTP` or `HTTPS`.

- **Return Type**: Select the type of data and how the HTTP Callout will respond. The available types are TEXT, NUM, and BOOL:
  - ○ TEXT: The returned value will be sent as a text string
  - ○ NUM: The returned value will be sent as a number
  - ○ BOOL: The returned value will be sent as a Boolean value

- **Expression to extract data from the response**: Define what will be sent back to the client, for example, HTTP.RES.BODY(200). This means that there will be 200 bytes sent back from the requested URL.

- **Cache Expiration Time (in secs)**: This is the duration in seconds for which the Callout response is cached. The cached responses will be stored in an integrated caching content group named calloutContentGroup. The integrated caching license is required for this functionality.

 Before configuring the HTTP Callout policy, be sure about what you want to configure. This is because we can't make changes to the HTTP Callout once it's configured except for the return type settings. So, we can't modify an expression that's configured.

After creating the HTTP Callout configuration, it's time to configure the responder policy, which will be needed to call the HTTP Callout. The responder policy can be configured globally or on the load balancing virtual server. The expression will be SYS.HTTP_CALLOUT(NAMEOFTHECREATEDHTTPCALLOUT). An explanation of the configured responder will be in the chapter.

For an HTTP Callout to work correctly, all the HTTP Callout parameters and the entities associated with the Callout must be configured correctly. While the NetScaler appliance does not check the validity of the HTTP Callout parameters, it indicates the state of the bound entities, namely the server or virtual server to which the HTTP Callout is sent. The following list shows you the icons and describes the conditions under which these icons are displayed:

⬤: The state of the server that hosts the HTTP Callout agent, or the load balancing, content switching, or cache redirection virtual server to which the HTTP Callout is sent is UP

⬤: The state of the server that hosts the HTTP Callout agent, or the load balancing, content switching, or cache redirection virtual server to which the HTTP Callout is sent is OUT OF SERVICE

Rate limiting

With the rate limiting feature in Citrix NetScaler, we can define a maximum load for load balancing virtual servers or configured backend servers. With this feature, we can configure so as to let Citrix NetScaler monitor the rate of traffic. Based on the configured rate limiting, Citrix NetScaler can block access for example. This monitoring feature is real-time. The rate limiting feature is especially useful when the network is under attack. So, with rate limiting, it's possible to prevent **Distributed Denial-of-Service (DDoS)** attacks. By using rate limiting, we can improve the reliability of the network and the resources that are presented by Citrix NetScaler.

Monitoring and controlling of the rate of traffic can be done based on:

- Virtual servers
- URLs
- Domains
- Combinations of URLs and domains
- User-defined expressions

With rate limiting, it's possible to throttle the traffic rate when it's too high. It's also possible to redirect traffic to another load balancing virtual server if it exceeds the configured limits. We can apply these rate-based monitors to HTTP, TCP, and DNS requests.

For every instance or request, it's possible to configure different limiters. The different options available will be described shortly.

In order to use limiters, we need filters to identify where the limit needs to be configured. These filters are called rate limiting selectors. A lot of predefined filters are already available, but if necessary, we can create a new one.

Rate limiting can be accessed using the following code in, for example, rewrite policies and responder policies:

```
SYS.CHECK.LIMIT(NAMEOFTHECREATEDRATELIMITIDENTIFIER)
```

Configuring rate limiting

Go to **AppExpert** | **Rate Limiting** | **Selectors** and click on **Add**. Fill in the correct information based on this explanation:

- **Name**: This will be the name where the rate limiting selector will be named to

- **Expressions**: This will be the expression used to identify where the rate limiting should filter, for example, `CLIENT.IP.SRC` or `HTTP.REQ.LB_VSERVER.NAME`

After we have created the selector, we will create the actual Limit Identifier. This Limit Identifier contains settings about the limit. Fill in the correct information based on the following explanation:

- **Name**: This will be the name where the Rate Limit Identifier will be named to.

- **Selector**: Choose the selector created in the preceding step, or select a predefined one.

- **Mode**: We can use `REQUEST_RATE`, `CONNECTION`, or `NONE`. With `REQUEST_RATE`, we monitor the requests/time slice; with `CONNECTION`, we monitor the active transactions; and with `NONE`, we don't define any type of traffic for tracking.

- **Limit Type**: This option will be available only when you are using `REQUEST_RATE`. With **Limit Type**, we can select two types: `SMOOTH` and `BURSTY`. With `SMOOTH`, we spread the permitted number of requests in a given interval of time in the configured time slice. With `BURSTY`, we only allow the maximum configured quota in the time slice.

- **Threshold**: This option allows the maximum number of requests in the configured time slice. When `REQUEST_RATE` is selected, the mode will be the maximum tracked requests. In the `CONNECTION` mode, this threshold will be the total number of allowed connections.

- **Time Slice**: This contains information about the time interval that will be used to verify that the threshold has been exceeded. The time will be in milliseconds.

- **Maximum Bandwidth**: This is the maximum permitted bandwidth in kbps.

- **Traps**: This is the number of traps that will be sent in the time slice by SNMP.

 Use the show `ns limitSessions <limitIdentifier>` code to show information about the configured rate limiting.

Policies and expressions

In a lot of Citrix NetScaler's features, we can use policies and expressions based on our requirements. Also, based on our requirements, we can make a difference depending on particular expressions. For example, it's possible to show different information for Windows clients and Mac OS X clients.

An expression can enable NetScaler to accomplish the following:

- Return the hostname in an HTTP request
- Determine the IP address of a client that sent a TCP request
- Identify the data that an HTTP request contains (for example, a popular spreadsheet or a word-processing application)
- Calculate the length of an HTTP request

Citrix NetScaler supports classic and default syntax policies and expressions. Based on the feature, Citrix NetScaler supports one or both of the syntaxes. The default syntax provides greater capabilities than the classic syntax. The default syntax policies enable us to use more enhancements with respect to analyzing data, so it's possible to analyze the HTTP headers of an HTTP request. It's also possible to perform more operations based on the policy rules.

In the following table, you will find all the features of Citrix NetScaler with the supported policy types:

Feature name	Policy type
System	Classic
DNS	Default
SSL	Classic and default
Compression	Classic and default
Integrated caching	Default
Responder/rewrite	Default
Protection features	Classic
Content switching	Classic and default
AAA – traffic management	Classic. However, there are exceptions: Traffic policies support only default syntax policies Authorization policies support both
Cache redirection	Classic
Application firewall	Classic and default

Feature name	Policy type
NetScaler Gateway and the clientless access function	Default
NetScaler Gateway	Classic

Policies are used to evaluate traffic. To perform an action based on the evaluated traffic, we need to create actions or profiles.

Actions enable us to configure settings that are particular to the evaluated policy. So, for example, it's possible to perform a particular action when we find an HTTP header in the request during evaluation of a policy.

Not all features support actions, but they use profiles. A profile contains a collection of settings for performing actions, for example, session policies in the NetScaler Gateway.

Citrix has a table with a complete summary of the use of actions and profiles in different NetScaler features. The table can be found at `http://docs.citrix.com/en-us/netscaler/11/appexpert/policies-and-expressions/ns-pi-intro-pol-exp-wrapper-con/ns-pi-adv-class-pol-con.html`.

Policy binding

In order to get the policy working, it has to be bound to a virtual server or a global level. As you can imagine, there are different bind locations possible; based on our needs, we can select the proper bind location.

The different bind locations are described as follows:

- **Global**:
    - **Request**: The policy will be available for all features when there is a request from a client or device
    - **Response**: The policy will be available for all features when there is a response from a client or device

- **Virtual Server**:
    - **Request**: The policy will be available for this particular virtual server when there is a request from a client or device, for example, a redirect to another URL when only the DNS name is entered.
    - **Response**: The policy will be available for this particular virtual server when there is a response from a client or device.

- **Policy label**: This is available for default syntax policies only. We can configure groups of policies by using policy labels. While using policy labels, we can create groups, which can be bound to services.

- **Other bind points**: For some of Citrix NetScaler's features, it's also possible to bind policies, for example, classic policies for the Citrix NetScaler Gateway for session policies.

Evaluation order

Classic policies, policy groups, and policies within a group are evaluated in a particular order depending on the following:

- **The bind location of the policy**: For example, global or for the virtual server.

- **The configured priority level**: For every available policy, we can configure priorities. Policies with the lowest priority value will be evaluated first.

Default syntax policies will be evaluated in the following order:

1. Request global override.

2. Request virtual server.

3. Request global default.

4. Response global override.

5. Response virtual server.

6. Response global default.

> Because default syntax policies are easier to understand and you need less knowledge of network protocols, you have the option to convert classic policies into default syntax policies for features that support default syntax policies, of course.
>
> The code would be `nspepi -e "<classic expression>"`. For example, `nspepi -e "REQ.HTTP.URL == /*.jpg"` would be `"HTTP.REQ.URL.REGEX_MATCH(re#/(.*)\.jpg#)"`.
>
> Also, some of Citrix NetScaler's features support both policies. Be aware that only one type of policy can be used for a feature.

Parsing policies

Default syntax policies have the advantage of parsing information of the HTTP, TCP, UDP, and SSL protocols. This information can be very useful for making decisions on what to show or hide. It's also possible to evaluate client **Secure Sockets Layer** (**SSL**) certificates based on the X.509 technology. Also, reading information about the HTTP protocol is possible. So, based on one of the HTTP headers, we can decide what the client can see. For example, the `User-Agent` header always contains information about the used web browser. As you may know, there are differences when visiting websites with different web browsers. Internet Explorer could give a totally different page layout than, for example, Google Chrome or Mozilla Firefox. By detecting this information, we can rewrite, for example, pages in order to make them work for all web browsers.

> More information and commands can be found at `http://docs.citrix.com/en-us/netscaler/11/appexpert/policies-and-expressions/ns-pi-adv-exp-pars-http-tcp-udp-data-wrapper-con.html` for HTTP, TCP, and UDP data. Refer to `http://docs.citrix.com/en-us/netscaler/11/appexpert/policies-and-expressions/ns-pi-ae-parse-ssl-certs-wrapper-con.html` for SSL certificates.

Rewrite

The rewrite feature is a very useful feature when Citrix NetScaler is used to publish HTTP/SSL or TCP information. This feature can be used for request or response traffic. Rewrite is very useful for hiding/removing configurations, appending the default page, custom HTTP errors, hiding HTTP headers, and so on.

The working of the rewrite feature

The rewrite feature requires a rule and an action to perform the required tasks. The rule is used to identify whether the rule needs to be applied. The configured action will perform the actual action—what we like to rewrite. It's possible to bind multiple rewrite policies on every bind point. Based on the priority, we can define what needs to be applied first if the rule matches the request.

The bind point could be at a global level or defined for a specific Citrix NetScaler load balancing or content switching virtual server.

The rewrite feature also has some default rewrites installed, and these can't be deleted.

The policies from the rewrite feature are followed according to these steps:

1. First, Citrix NetScaler will check for global policies.

2. After the global policies, Citrix NetScaler will verify the policies at the bind point. If there are multiple policies, then Citrix NetScaler will evaluate the policies based on the configured priority. The lowest priority will be evaluated first. This policy will be evaluated. If the policy matches, Citrix NetScaler will add the rule to the list of performing actions.

3. After all the evaluated policies are walked through, the listed actions will be conducted.

The GoTo expression

While adding the rewrite policy to the bind point, there is the GoTo expression, which can be filled in. The default is the END function. The options available are as follows:

*   **END**: Evaluation after the policy will be ended. This means that no policy will be evaluated after this one.

*   **NEXT**: The next available policy will be evaluated, if it exists.

*   **USE_INVOCATION_RESULT**: GoTo **END** or **NEXT** based on the results of the invocation list.

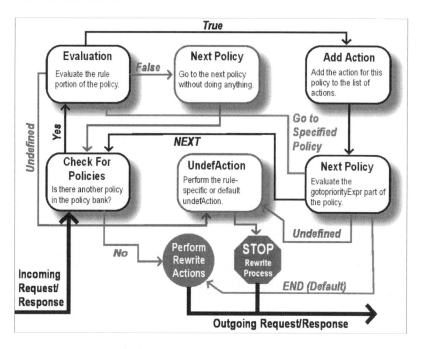

The preceding diagram describes the flowchart of the rewrite feature.

Rewrite actions

Citrix NetScaler has a lot of actions available for performing actions. The most commonly used action will be explained as follows:

Rewrite action type	Expression to choose target location	Argument
INSERT_HTTP_HEADER: Inserts the HTTP header that we like to insert.	The HTTP header that we like to insert.	The expression that describes the contents of the HTTP header that needs to be inserted.
INSERT_BEFORE: Inserts a new string before the target location.	The expression that contains information on where the action needs to be evaluated.	The text that needs to be added before the target location.
INSERT_AFTER: Inserts a new string after the target location.	The expression that contains information on where the action needs to be evaluated.	The text that needs to be added after the target location.
REPLACE: Replaces the designated string with a different string.	The expression that contains information on where the action needs to be evaluated.	The text that needs to be replaced by the target location expression.
DELETE: Deletes the designated information.	A string expression that describes what needs to be deleted.	
DELETE_HTTP_HEADER: Deletes the designated HTTP header.	The name of the HTTP header that we want to delete.	
CORRUPT_HTTP_HEADER: Replaces the name of the HTTP header with a corrupted name. If this type is used, the receiver can't recognize this HTTP header.	The name of the HTTP header that we don't want visible on the receiver side.	
REPLACE_HTTP_RES: Replaces the HTTP response.	The matching expression that needs to be sent back. This will be an HTTP response.	
REPLACE_ALL: Replaces all the designated strings with a different string.	The expression that contains information on where the action needs to be evaluated.	All of the text that needs to be replaced by the target location expression.

Rewrite action type	Expression to choose target location	Argument
DELETE_ALL: Delete every occurrence that matches the target location.	A string expression that describes what needs to be deleted.	
INSERT_AFTER_ALL: Inserts a new string after the target location. This will be used to insert for all the matching target locations rather than just the first match.	The expression that contains information on where the action needs to be evaluated.	The text that needs to be added after the target location.
INSERT_BEFORE_ALL: Inserts a new string before the target location.	The expression that contains information on where the action needs to be evaluated.	The text that needs to be added before the target location.

Configuring a rewrite policy

Go to **AppExpert | Rewrite | Actions** and click on **Add**. Fill in the correct information based on the following explanation:

- **Name**: This will be the name where the rewrite actions will be named to.
- **Type**: Select the rewrite type that you want to perform. The most commonly used types have been described previously.

  Depending on the type, there will be an extra field that needs to be filled in.
- **Comments**: Fill in comments if necessary.

Now the action is done, and we need to create a policy.

Go to **AppExpert | Rewrite | Policies** and click on **Add**. Fill in the correct information based on the explanation given here:

- **Name**: This will be the name where the rewrite actions will be named to
- **Action**: There are different options here, as follows:
  - Insert: The rewrite action that we created earlier. All rewrite actions will be visible.
  - NOREWRITE: The request or response will not be rewritten.
  - RESET: The connection will be aborted at the TCP level.
  - DROP: The message will be dropped.

- **Log action**: When the rewrite policy matches, it's possible to log the action to an SNMP server or the syslog of Citrix NetScaler

- **Undefined-Result Action**: When an error occurs, for some reason, Citrix NetScaler will perform the selected action

- **Expression**: Configure the expression that Citrix NetScaler needs to check whether the action needs to be processed

- **Comments**: Fill in comments if necessary

After these steps, we can bind the policy to the global level or a specific Citrix NetScaler virtual server.

Responder

The response feature in Citrix NetScaler is very useful for responding to HTTP requests. When a user connects from an untrusted location, we like to block access. For example, we send another language to display based on the location or redirect to a secure connection based on HTTPs.

The responder feature can handle responses based on who sends the request, where it is sent from, and other criteria.

Configuring a responder policy

To create a responder policy, we need to start by creating the responder action.

Go to **AppExpert** | **Responder** | **Actions** and click on **Add**. Fill in the correct information based on the following explanation:

- **Name**: This will be the name where the responder actions will be named to

- **Type**: Select the responder type that you would like to perform:
    - NOOP: This type aborts the action but doesn't alter the packet flow. So, if there are multiple responder policies configured, Citrix NetScaler will to go the next policy and unmark the current one.

    - Respond with: This sends a response configured in the expression, without which the request will be forwarded to the web server behind. Citrix NetScaler will act as a web server and can be used to send a simple request back, for example, blocking access for specific IP addresses and sending a web page that the IP address is not authorized.

- ○ `Redirect`: Redirect the request to another web page or web server. For example, redirect `http` to `https`.

- ○ `Respond with SQL OK`: Respond with a `SQL OK` response to a SQL query. The expression will be the `SQL OK` that will be sent.

- ○ `Respond with SQL Error`: Respond with a `SQL Error` response to a SQL query. The expression will be the SQL error that will be sent.

- ○ `Respond with HTML page`: Respond with a custom HTML page. So, we can make, for example, a maintenance page and show it.

- **Comments**: Fill in comments, if necessary

> The expression in the responder action always contains information about what needs to be sent back to the client. For example, if we wish to use the redirect functionality to perform `http` to `https`, then the expression would be `"https://" + HTTP.REQ.HOSTNAME + HTTP.REQ.URL.PATH_AND_QUERY`.
>
> `HTTP.REQ.HOSTNAME` contains the actual hostname that the client has filled in. `HTTP.REQ.URL.PATH_AND_QUERY` contains information on what was filled in behind the / sign. For example, `http://websites.com/images/frontpage/header.png` would be `https://websites.com/images/frontpage/header.png`.

After creating the action, we need to create the policy.

Navigate to **AppExpert | Responder | Policies** and click on **Add**. Fill in the correct information based on the following explanation:

- **Name**: This will be the name where the rewrite actions will be named to

- **Action**: There are different options here, as follows:
    - ○ NOOP: This type aborts the action but doesn't alter the packet flow. So, if there are multiple responder policies configured, Citrix NetScaler will to go the next policy and unmark this one.
    - ○ RESET: The connection will be aborted at the TCP level.
    - ○ DROP: The message will be dropped.

- **Log action**: When the rewrite policy matches, it's possible to log the action to an SNMP server or to the syslog of Citrix NetScaler

- **Undefined-Result Action**: When an error occurs, for some reason, Citrix NetScaler will perform the selected action

- **Expression**: Configure the expression that Citrix NetScaler needs to check whether the action needs to be processed

- **Comments**: Fill in comments, if necessary

 You can verify the policy from the CLI using `show responder policy <name>`.

Because the responder policy is a default expression, it's possible to get more information by analyzing the data. So, it's possible to look into the entire HTTP request. In this way, it's possible to use an expression with `CLIENT.IP.SRC`, for example. Thus, based on the source IP address of the client, we can bind the action.

 As explained in the above sections, it's possible to halt the responder or rewrite policies by using HTTP Callout. Using `SYS.HTTP_CALLOUT(<name>)`, we can perform the HTTP Callout functionality.

Rewrite versus responder

The responder feature is very useful for resetting or dropping a connection based on client information, responding to another website, or responding with a custom message. For all other functionalities, it's better to use the rewrite feature. The rewrite feature can manipulate traffic and hide information when necessary.

Summary

This chapter described the most commonly used AppExpert features of Citrix NetScaler. All of these features are one of the benefits of using Citrix NetScaler, because all of them are available in one appliance. Also, the rewrite/responder feature is very useful when using Citrix NetScaler (also as a reserve proxy). Using these features, we can add more security to the environment, and only the necessary information can be made visible to the clients.

In the next chapter, we will describe integration with Citrix components in combination with the Citrix NetScaler appliance. These components are useful if you want to achieve a complete infrastructure and get proper information about the clients.

3

Integration with Citrix® Components

Besides Citrix NetScaler, Citrix also has a lot of other components that can interact with Citrix NetScaler. The components can be used separately from each other. The different components will be described in this chapter.

NetScaler® Insight Center

Citrix NetScaler Insight Center will be used to monitor and report on Citrix NetScaler and Citrix CloudBridge appliances. Citrix NetScaler Insight Center can be used for Web Insight, HDX Insight, and for WAN Insight. Web Insight will be used for HTTP analytics, HDX Insight will be used for monitoring ICA traffic and WAN Insight will give us information about the efficiency of the optimized traffic. Also Citrix NetScaler Insight Center will be used to monitor, diagnose, and subsequently improve the performance of business-critical applications and is essential to ensuring a positive user experience and maintaining the highest levels of employee productivity and customer satisfaction.

Licensing

Depending on the configured Citrix NetScaler license, Insight Center will save the information.

The following table describes Web Insight license/version information. As you can see, Web Insight is free and doesn't require a special license to get information from HTTP traffic. The other table will describe the license structure for HDX Insight. To collect information from ICA traffic, we need at least a Citrix NetScaler Enterprise license. The limitation of the Enterprise license is a maximum duration of 1 hour, which means that we only can see ICA traffic monitoring from 1 hour ago.

License/ Version	9.3	10	10.1	10.5
Standard	ⓘ	ⓘ	✔	✔
Enterprise	ⓘ	ⓘ	✔	✔
Platinum	ⓘ	✔	✔	✔

License/Duration	5 minutes	1 Hour	1 Day	1 Week	1 Month
Standard	✖	✖	✖	✖	✖
Enterprise	✔	✔	✖	✖	✖
Platinum	✔	✔	✔	✔	✔

WAN Insight doesn't require any additional license.

To gather information, we need to enable data collection to follow traffic through the Citrix NetScaler or Citrix CloudBridge appliances. Insight Center is capable of gathering information from load balancing virtual servers, content switching virtual servers, NetScaler Gateway virtual servers, and from the cache redirection feature.

Reporting

This section will describe the different report functionalities available in the Citrix Insight Center.

Web Insight

Web Insight will be used to gather information about the HTTP traffic that's passing through Citrix NetScaler. The information will be visible in reports. These reports are created automatically in Insight Center. These reports for Web Insight contains information about the several entities:

- **Devices**: Show information about the number of requests received by Citrix NetScaler appliances based on the client device
- **Applications**: Show information about the contacted application for all the configured Citrix NetScaler appliances accessed by the client
- **Domains**: Display information about all the contacted domains accessed by the client

To gather all the information it's necessary to use the cache redirection feature in Citrix NetScaler. By enabling this feature, Insight Center can build relationships between the different information.

In the following URL all Web Insight metrics are displayed with the different license information. `http://docs.citrix.com/en-us/netscaler-insight/11-0/viewing-reports/ni-viewing-web-insight-reports-ref.html`.

HDX Insight

HDX Insight will be used for analyzing ICA traffic through Citrix NetScaler. HDX Insight gives the Citrix XenApp/XenDesktop engineer a good view about the traffic used by the ICA protocol. Besides the information, it's very easy to indicate traffic problems, for example a slow response for remote users. One of the metrics is WAN latency. This metric will show the average latency caused on the client device network. Of course HDX Insight provides a lot more information that can be used for troubleshooting. NetScaler Insight Center subsequently compiles and presents HDX Insight data obtained from NetScaler, providing IT administrators with unparalleled visibility into their virtual desktop/application environment. The metrics that HDX Insight features will report can be found here: `http://docs.citrix.com/en-us/netscaler-insight/11-0/viewing-reports/ni-viewing-hdx-reports-ref.html` and `https://www.citrix.com/content/dam/citrix/en_us/documents/products-solutions/hdx-insight-powered-by-citrix-netscaler-insight-center.pdf`.

WAN Insight

WAN Insight will be used to gather information about the traffic through Citrix CloudBridge. This information could be very useful to get information about the traffic flowing through Citrix CloudBridge. WAN Insight metrics can be find in the following table:

Metric name	Description
Average RTT (ms) (WAN latency)	Delay in milliseconds that the user experiences while interacting with an application
Compression Ratio	Data compression ratio achieved between the branch office and datacenter appliances in a particular duration
Bytes Sent over WAN	Number of bytes that the CloudBridge appliance sends over the WAN network
Bytes Received Over WAN	Number of bytes that the CloudBridge appliance receives from the WAN network
Active Accelerated Connections	Number of active WAN connections being accelerated
Active Unaccelerated Connections	Number of active WAN connections not being accelerated
Packets Sent	Number of packets that the CloudBridge appliance sends over the network
Packets Received	Number of packets that the CloudBridge appliance receives from the network
LAN RTO	Number of times the CloudBridge appliance has timed out retransmission to the LAN network
WAN RTO	Number of times the CloudBridge appliance has timed out retransmission to the WAN network
Retransmit Packets (LAN)	Number of packets the CloudBridge appliance retransmitted to the LAN network
Retransmit Packets (WAN)	Number of packets the CloudBridge appliance retransmitted to the WAN network

Installation

Installation of the Citrix Insight Center is very easy, because Citrix delivers ready implementation templates that are available for Microsoft Hyper-V, Citrix XenServer, or VMware ESX. The requirements for all the hypervisors are shown in the next table.

Component	Requirement
RAM	3 GB or more
Virtual CPU	2 or more
Storage space	120 GB required
Virtual Network Interfaces	1
Throughput	1 Gbps or 100 Mbps

 Select the proper storage space because you can't increase the disk size afterwards.

The prerequisites for Citrix NetScaler are:

- **NSIP**: Add NS using NSIP not SNIP

- **NetScaler State**: The state of NetScaler has to be UP before adding it to Insight

- **nCore**: Only nCore NetScaler appliances

- **Standalone NetScaler Gateway**: You cannot add and get reports over the Standalone NetScaler Gateway™ appliance on Insight

- **HA**: For NetScaler HA deployment, add both NetScaler appliances on Insight to get reports across both the nodes

- **Cluster**: You can't monitor NetScaler cluster deployment on Insight

- **HTTP/HTTPS**: Make sure that both the NetScaler appliance and the NetScaler Insight Center appliance have either HTTP access or HTTPS access enabled

- **NS user**: The user added while adding NetScaler on Insight should have write-level access to NetScaler

- **NTP**: If you want to use NTP server time on the NetScaler Insight Center, make sure that you configure NTP before enabling AppFlow on the virtual servers

- **ICA**: Set the ICA session time-out value on Insight

- **HDX Insight**: Double hop and session reliability is supported from NetScaler Release 10.5 build 10.5 onwards

After the first boot, we need to follow some steps to configure the Citrix Insight Center with an IP address, default gateway, and so on. After hitting the **Save and Quit** menu item we need to select a deployment type. There are four different options:

- **NetScaler Insight Server**: This will be the actual NetScaler Insight Server. This option will be used when this node is the first NetScaler Insight Center in your network.

- **NetScaler Insight Agent**: The NetScaler Insight Agent will be used for processing HTTP traffic from Citrix NetScaler. There could be more than one NetScaler Insight Agent configured.

- **Connector Node**: The Connector Node will be used to distribute the data to the database nodes that will be received from the NetScaler Insight Agents.

- **Database Node**: The Database Node will be used to store data from the received NetScaler or CloudBridge appliance. We can install multiple database nodes.

```
   1. NetScaler Insight Server.
   2. Connector Node.
   3. Database Node.
   4. NetScaler Insight Agent.
   5. Cancel and quit.

Select a choice from 1 to 5 [5]: ▌
```

When Citrix Insight Center is started we can connect to it by browsing to the configured IP address in the first step with a Web browser. We can log in with the default username and password on the Citrix Insight Center with username `nsroot` and password `nsroot`.

After login, the welcome screen appears. Here we can add Citrix NetScaler or Citrix CloudBridge. We need the IP address of NetScaler or the IP address from Citrix CloudBridge. After the Wizard is completed, it's possible to add more devices if necessary.

This IP address should be the IP address that has management access enabled. We have to make sure that we add all Citrix NetScaler and Citrix CloudBridge appliances in order to get full monitoring and analytics.

In the next step we can select the actual load balancing, content switching, VPN, or the cache redirection virtual server we want to monitor by Citrix Insight Center.

When enabling **Enable Geo data collection for Web and HDX Insight**, all the client IP addresses will be collected to determine the location of the client. In order to support geo data collection we should upload a geo data collection database; this can be done later in the configuration.

Sending data to the NetScaler Insight Center will be done by the AppFlow feature. AppFlow connects to the NetScaler Insight Server on port UDP 4739. In order to receive data we need AppFlow enabled for the virtual server. In this case we may like to enable HDX Insight. So select in the **Application List** the **VPN** view. Select the NetScaler Gateway virtual server and select **Enable AppFlow**.

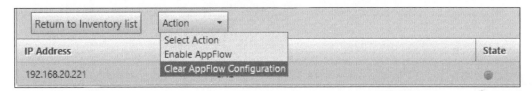

 When Citrix NetScaler is in another network, Citrix NetScaler Insight Center should ensure sure that the NetScaler IP has access to the Citrix NetScaler Insight Center IP address on port UDP 4739.

The **Enable AppFlow** dialog will pop up to create an expression. In the most cases this will be the `true` value, but we can also create a custom expression. For example `CLIENT.IP.SRC.IN_SUBNET(192.20.0.0/16)` if you want only internal address for analytics.

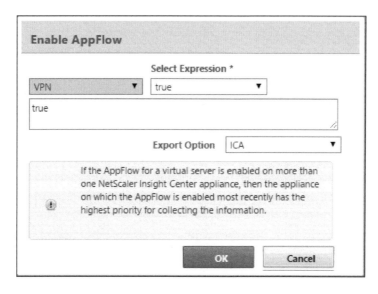

After pressing **OK** the NetScaler Gateway virtual server will be monitored and the data will be sent to the Citrix Insight Server when the expression matches.

Configuration

Adding more Citrix NetScaler or Citrix CloudBridge appliances can be done under the **Configuration** tab. Click on **Inventory** to add more appliances if necessary.

Citrix Insight Center can be accessed by HTTP or by HTTPS traffic. When using secure access it's possible to upload your own certificate. If you use the default certificate we always get a warning in the browser that the certificate isn't trusted because it's a self-signed certificate. So it's easier to replace the certificate with a trusted certificate authority.

 If you only need secure access to the Citrix Insight Center then go to **Configuration**, change **System Settings** and enable the **Secure Access only** checkbox. This checkbox can only be set if you connected through a secure connection.

The communication between the monitored devices and Citrix NetScaler Insight Center will by default be done based on HTTP. It's possible to change this to HTTPS. This can be done under **Configuration, Change System Settings** and change the drop-down box from `http` to `https`. After pressing **OK** the communication will be done securely.

System menu

In the **System** menu there are a lot of things to configure, as follows:

- **Change Time Zone**: Here you can modify the time zone from Citrix NetScaler Insight Center. Please make sure that the Citrix NetScaler/Citrix CloudBridge appliance has the same time configured as Citrix NetScaler Insight Center. You can configure a NTP server.

- **Change Hostname**: Here you can modify the hostname of Citrix NetScaler Insight Center.

- **Change System Settings**: Here you can modify the security settings as explained earlier.

- **Change SSL Settings**: Enable or disable specific SSL/TLS protocols. For security reasons it's best practice to disable SSLv3 and also disable SSL renegotiation. For more information see this Citrix article: `http://support.citrix.com/article/CTX123359`.

- **Change ICA Session Timeout**: Time period for which an ICA session can remain in the idle state before being terminated.

- **Configure Multihop feature**: Enable the checkbox when using a multihop Citrix NetScaler environment.

- **Change Database Cache Settings**: Here it's possible to make database cache adjustments. By default the database will be cached on Citrix NetScaler Insight Server.

- **Change Data Record Log Settings**: Data record logs provide information about AppFlow records. These logs are useful for troubleshooting but aren't necessary when Citrix NetScaler Insight Center is working. By default the logs for HDX Insight and Citrix CloudBridge are enabled.

- **Change URL Parameter Settings**: If the URLs captured by Web Insight are very long, we can enable the **Trim URL** option. URLs will be trimmed for better visibility.

- **Change Database Cleanup Settings**: When a lot of information is captured, the database size will increase a lot. Enabling the database cleanup option will remove out-of-date data from the database.

- **Change Database Index Settings**: By default the index setting is enabled. With enabled, index setting database queries are more efficient.
- **Change Adaptive Threshold Settings**: The adaptive threshold can be enabled to set the threshold value for the maximum number of hits on each URL. If the maximum number of hits on a URL is greater than the threshold value set for the URL, a syslog message will be sent to an external syslog server.
- **Change Web Insight Report Settings**: Select the entities that need to be visible in the reports on the dashboard.
- **Limit Data Duration Persistency**: Here we can configure the number of days the generated reports can persist in the database.
- **Change URL Data Collection Settings**: Disable URL data collection if you don't want to display the URL reports on Web Insight node.
- **Change Dashboard Reporting Time Zone Settings**: The reports on the dashboard display your local time by default. Select GMT if you want them to display the GMT time zone.

Authentication

By default the Citrix NetScaler Insight Center authentication method uses the LOCAL user database. Citrix NetScaler Insight Center also supports external authentication services such as LDAP, RADIUS, and TACACS. The configuration is the same on Citrix NetScaler. But if we want LDAP authentication as the default we need to change the default value.

1. Navigate to **System | Authentication**.
2. Click **Authentication Configuration**.
3. Set the following parameters:
    - **Server Type**: Type of authentication server configured for user authentication
    - **Server Name**: Name of the authentication server configured
    - **Enable fallback local authentication**: This functionality can be enabled if you like to have support for local authentication when the external authentication fails
4. Click **OK**.

Insight deployment management

Insight deployment management will be used to add more agents, connectors, and database nodes because, if we want to save a lot of information, there should be enough resources to actually save it. In the menu it's possible to add a maximum amount of data received per minute for each different function and to change the maximum number of days that the data will be stored in the database. It's a best practice to make no changes to the ICA traffic settings.

Thresholds

It's possible via threshold and alert configurations to send notifications by e-mail or through SMS when a threshold or alert matches. So for example when the DC latency (ms) is above a special value an alert will be sent to the administrator. This makes it very easy to determine issues in the environment.

Updating NetScaler® Insight Center

Citrix delivers updates for Citrix NetScaler Insight Center every time there is a firmware update for the Citrix NetScaler appliance. This new build could contain bug fixes or new features. Before upgrading Citrix NetScaler Insight Center, please make sure you update the Citrix NetScaler appliances first.

The update scenario is as follows:

1. Download the latest build from the Citrix website.
2. Navigate to **System**.
3. Click **Upgrade NetScaler Insight Center**.
4. Click **Browse** and browse to the path where you saved the download.
5. Click **OK**.
6. Click **Yes**.

The build will be uploaded and installed. After the reboot Citrix NetScaler Insight Center contains the build we uploaded in the previous steps.

Troubleshooting

Citrix NetScaler Insight Center logs a lot of information by default in the log files on the appliances. These can be very useful to determine issues with connection or information.

 Citrix has some very good and useful troubleshooting tips available. These troubleshooting tips can be found here: `http://docs.citrix.com/en-us/netscaler-insight/11-0/ni-troubleshoot-tips-ref.html`.

CloudBridge™

Citrix CloudBridge accelerates application delivery across public and private cloud networks, and provides enterprises with the unique ability to support WAN virtualization. Combined with visibility into application performance, CloudBridge allows enterprises to evolve toward software-defined WANs for hybrid networking.

Citrix CloudBridge can be a virtual or a physical appliance. To get optimization working we need a datacenter on the Citrix CloudBridge appliance and also on the branch office of Citrix CloudBridge, because the traffic that was optimized also needs to be deoptimized. If an appliance on the branch office isn't feasible, we could install the Citrix CloudBridge Plug-in on the end user device. This plug-in is only available for Microsoft Windows endpoints. This solution can reduce the cost of delivering mobile workspaces to local branches by up to 80 percent, while realizing virtually 100 percent availability for high-priority applications.

Citrix CloudBridge has a lot of different models; depending on the needs of the services we can decide to use a virtual appliance or a physical one. The virtual appliance will be better for smaller sites but requires more configuration. The three new CloudBridge models—VPX 50, VPX 100, and VPX 200—offer an expanded set of high end VPX options that provide a higher scale for datacenter deployments in a software-defined datacenter. The VPX 6 model offers an additional option for branch office deployments. The new CloudBridge 1000WS series is the latest in a line of proven appliances for the branch office.

Citrix CloudBridge is especially useful for companies with a lot of branch offices with a small Internet or MPLS throughput. By implementing Citrix CloudBridge we can optimize traffic, cache traffic, or perform protocol acceleration for CIFS, ICA, Microsoft Outlook (MAPI), and SSL traffic. Also it's possible to use the traffic shaping feature; with this feature we can use **Quality of Service (QoS)** to prioritize traffic.

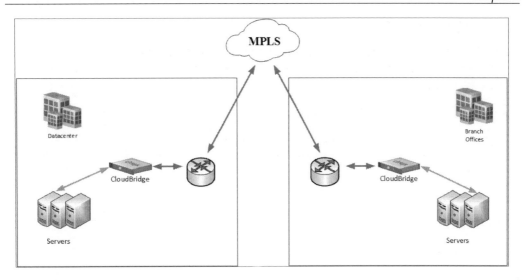

Appliances

There are different appliances available for Citrix CloudBridge. Virtual appliances are available for Microsoft Hyper-V, VMware ESX, or Citrix XenServer. The physical appliances are there in different capacities. Choosing the perfect appliance will be based on link capacity, user capacity, and disk capacity.

When we have a lot of branch offices it's better to implement a physical appliance at the datacenter. The physical appliance is capable of handling all the traffic of the branch offices without having performance issues, because the appliance is dedicated and has dedicated hardware available for caching, rendering, and so on.

Link capacity

The most important factor when selecting a Citrix CloudBridge appliance is support for the WAN connection. Your chosen appliance should at least be able to handle all traffic passing through the WAN connection. So if your WAN connection has a 20 Mbps link speed, Citrix CloudBridge should also support at least a 20 Mbps link speed.

User capacity

With user capacity Citrix means the maximum number XenApp/XenDesktop concurrent users. This value should not be exceeded when the appliance needs to optimize this sort of traffic. If you don't use XenApp/XenDesktop optimization, the value should the number of users of other appliances passing Citrix CloudBridge.

Disk capacity

The disk space will be used for caching of traffic and compression history. Adding more disk space will result in a greater compression performance.

Deployment modes

Citrix CloudBridge needs to be able to see the traffic flowing between the datacenter and the branch offices. In order to see the traffic, Citrix CloudBridge can be placed in different modes depending on the network infrastructure.

The different modes are:

- **Inline mode**: This mode provides the highest performance. All the data flows in on one accelerated Ethernet port and out on the other Ethernet port.

- **Inline with dual bridges**: The same as inline mode but with two independent accelerated connections.

- **WCCP mode**: This mode is recommended when inline mode is not practical. This mode requires the support of your router/firewall.

- **Virtual inline mode**: Similar to WCCP but uses policy-based routing. Requires a dedicated LAN port on the router/firewall.

- **Group mode**: Two or more inline appliances, one per link, within a site. Recommended only when all other modes don't fit.

- **High-availability mode**: Combine two inline or virtual inline appliances into a high-availability pair. The primary appliance will handle all the traffic. If the primary appliance fails, the secondary appliance will be the new primary. This mode requires an appliance with an Ethernet bypass card.

- **Transparent mode**: The recommended mode for communication with the Citrix CloudBridge Plug-in.

- **Redirector mode**: Used by the CloudBridge Plug-in to forward traffic to the appliance. *This mode isn't recommended.*

The inline modes aren't recommended when Citrix CloudBridge appliances don't have an Ethernet bypass card.

When Citrix CloudBridge stops responding, all the traffic will be sent to the appliance, but the appliance won't send it through. When the appliance has an Ethernet Bypass card all the traffic will still flow through Citrix CloudBridge but won't be optimized. No Ethernet bypass card means a *single point of failure*.

CloudBridge™ Connector

Citrix CloudBridge Connector is a feature of the Citrix CloudBridge appliance that connects datacenters to external clouds and hosting environments. By using Citrix CloudBridge Connector the appliance will make the external cloud a secure extension of your own datacenter. The cloud-hosted environment will appear as if it's running in the same network as your own datacenter. Installing Citrix CloudBridge in the cloud as well will result in a WAN optimized connection between the datacenter and the cloud.

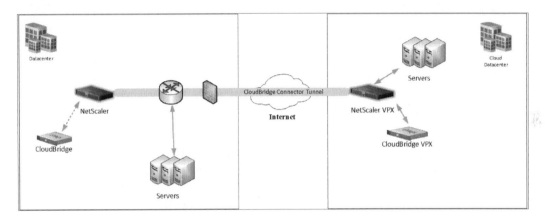

The preceding screenshot demonstrates a basic configuration for connecting a **Cloud Datacenter** with the private datacenter. All traffic intended for the **Cloud Datacenter** will be sent through Citrix CloudBridge Connector. Citrix CloudBridge Connector is a secure connection based on IPsec with the GRE protocol. When it arrives at the **Cloud Datacenter** Citrix NetScaler decapsulates the packet by removing the GRE header. Citrix NetScaler will forward the traffic to Citrix CloudBridge, which applies the WAN optimization-related processes and sends the package back to Citrix NetScaler. Now the package looks the same as the server in the datacenter. The package has the destination IP of the server in the **Cloud Datacenter**, so Citrix NetScaler will send the package to the server.

The server in the **Cloud Datacenter** will process the request package and sends out a response packet. The destination IP will be the IP address of the server in the datacenter.

Installation

After selecting the best matching deployment modes, it's time to start the installation. It always starts with configuration of the management interface for physical appliances or the accelerated bridge port for the virtual appliance.

The default management IP of the physical appliance is 192.168.100.1.

Some of the deployment modes require additional configuration settings in the Citrix CloudBridge appliance; for example, WCCP needs to be enabled as a feature before WCCP is supported.

In order to use the Citrix CloudBridge features, we need to install the license. The license could be installed on the appliance or from the Citrix License Server configured in your network.

 If your Citrix CloudBridge can access your Citrix License Server please use the remote license server. By using the Citrix License Server, all licenses are in one place instead of being installed on every appliance. This makes the renewal of the license far easier.

The license file will be registered on the host ID. This host ID can be found in the Citrix CloudBridge appliance. After a reboot, the features are available and ready for configuring.

Compression

The compression technology from Citrix CloudBridge can be enabled as a feature. The built-in compression algorithm scans the data. In the data Citrix CloudBridge will search for strings of data that match strings that have sent before. When there is no match the data will be sent from the original source. If there is a match the compressed data will be sent to the destination. So it could be possible that gigabytes of data can be represented by a pointer that contains only a few bytes. Only those few bytes will be sent over the connection.

The compression engine is limited by the configured and available size of the compression history. The traditional compression algorithms in the Citrix CloudBridge appliance use compression histories of 64 KB or less. So, the more matches the compression algorithms can find, the better the compression ratio will be.

One of the advantages of a large compression history is that precompressed data will be compressed easily again with Citrix CloudBridge. A PNG image, for example, isn't compressed the first time. But whenever the file needs to be sent again the entire transfer is reduced to just the compression information, even if the file is sent by different users or with different protocols.

Normally, encrypted traffic can't be compressed because of the security layer, but Citrix CloudBridge can compress encrypted connection when Citrix CloudBridge is part of the security infrastructure. Citrix CloudBridge will join the security infrastructure automatically with Citrix XenApp/XenDesktop, SSL, CIFS, and MAPI joined manually.

Encrypted traffic acceleration

As we said in the previous chapter, encrypted traffic can't be accelerated by default because Citrix CloudBridge can't look into the package. So by default Citrix CloudBridge appliance isn't capable of optimizing CIFS, SMB, MAPI, and SSL traffic.

To get access to the CIFS, SMB, and MAPI secure traffic we need to configure Citrix CloudBridge as a member of the domain. Citrix CloudBridge can't be an actual member server but with the right configuration Citrix CloudBridge can see the encrypted traffic through a created delegated user in the Active Directory. This delegated user needs special permission. The configuration of the delegated user can be found here: `http://support.citrix.com/proddocs/topic/cloudbridge-74/cb-conf-sec-win-traffic-con.html`.

If we don't configure the Citrix CloudBridge appliance with a delegated user, CIFS, SMB, and MAPI encrypted traffic can't be accelerated.

 It's possible to accelerate CIFS/SMB traffic by disabling CIFS signing but this isn't a best practice.

CIFS acceleration has three parts:

- **TCP flow-control acceleration**: This is performed on all accelerated CIFS connections, regardless of protocol version.
- **CIFS protocol acceleration**: This optimization functionality increases the CIFS performance by reducing the number of round-trips needed for running a CIFS command. These optimizations are performed automatically on SMB1 and SMB2 CIFS connections.

- **CIFS compression**: CIFS connections are compressed automatically whenever they meet the requirements.

SMB version	TCP flow control	Compression	Protocol acceleration
Signing disabled			
SMB 1.0	Y	Y	Y
SMB 2.0	Y	Y	Y
SMB 2.1	Y	Y	N
SMB 3.0	Y	Y	N
Signing enabled, CloudBridge has joined domain			
SMB 1.0	Y	Y	Y
SMB 2.0	Y	Y	Y
SMB 2.1	Y	Y	N
SMB 3.0	Y	Y	N
Signing enabled, CloudBridge has not joined domain			
SMB 1.0	Y	N	N
SMB 2.0	Y	N	N
SMB 2.1	Y	N	N
SMB 3.0	Y	N	N

SSL compression

SSL compression is also one of the supported features. SSL compression can be configured with two modes: transparent proxy or split proxy.

- **SSL transparent proxy**: In this mode the server-side appliance (the appliance closest to the server) will act as the server. The SSL server private keys are installed on Citrix CloudBridge appliance. This mode supports client authentication, but Temp RSA and Diffie-Hellman aren't supported.

- **SSL split proxy**: In this mode the server-side appliance will act as the server to the client, and as a client to the server. The SSL server private keys are installed on the server-side appliance to allow it to act on the server's behalf.

Traffic shaping

Traffic shaping is a sort of Quality of Service (QoS) for link connections. For a lot of MPLS/WAN connections, QoS is very expensive or impossible to enable. When using Citrix CloudBridge it's possible to have QoS. The traffic shaping feature is highly configurable when necessary, but the default settings are fine in the most circumstances.

Traffic shaping is based on bandwidth-limited fair queuing. The feature applies policies to determine the right mix of traffic. Every traffic connection has a policy configured. The traffic shaping policy will be examined in a three-stage process:

1. The traffic will be examined by the application classifier to determine the type of application.
2. The application is looked up in the service-class list.
3. Finally, the policy will get the configured priority and other parameters for this traffic.

XenApp®/XenDesktop® acceleration

XenApp/XenDesktop acceleration uses three components:

- **Compression**: The Citrix CloudBridge appliance cooperates with XenApp and XenDesktop clients and servers to compress the data streams for interactive data (such as: mouse, keyboard, display, and audio) and batch data (printing and file transfers). XenApp/XenDesktop compression requires no configuration changes on the Citrix CloudBridge appliance.

- **Multistream ICA**: The Citrix CloudBridge appliance has support for the Multistream ICA protocol. This multistream ICA protocol can be enabled on the Citrix XenApp/XenDesktop environment as well as on the Citrix CloudBridge appliance. When the multistream ICA protocol is enabled, the ICA protocol will be split into four different connections; this provides better responsiveness and priority definition.

- **Traffic shaping**: Citrix CloudBridge traffic shaping uses the priority settings in the Citrix XenApp/XenDesktop data protocols. It's possible to adjust the priority of all the available virtual channels of the ICA protocol. So it's possible to give the file transfer channel a lower priority than for example the display virtual channel.

The Citrix® Command Center

The Citrix Command Center will be used to manage and monitor all Citrix NetScaler, Citrix NetScaler SDX platform, and Citrix CloudBridge appliances.

The Citrix Command Center delivers a unified console for management, and also provides the IT engineer/manager with real-time performance monitoring for Citrix NetScaler and Citrix CloudBridge environments. Some of the benefits are:

*   Centralized management of a NetScaler infrastructure
*   Automated configuration for multiple systems
*   Advanced performance monitoring and reporting
*   Global management of system events and alarms
*   Delegated user administration with complete audit information
*   Centralized SSL certificate management
*   Centralized change management

Besides monitoring, the Citrix Command Center allows IT engineers to easily manage multiple devices, whether the appliances are distributed globally or reside in a datacenter. With the Citrix Command Center we can easily create management tasks that need to be run often. Also the Command Center provides central monitoring of the health and performance of the appliance in the environment.

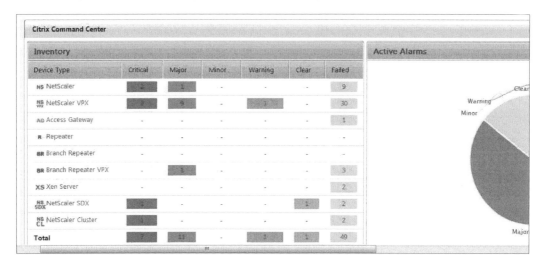

Software

The Citrix Command Center can be delivered as a software installation executable. The software can be installed on different Microsoft Windows servers and on Linux servers. Besides the software installation, the Citrix Command Center needs a database server. This database server will be used to save the performance monitoring and all other settings/functionality around the Citrix Command Center.

The supported operating systems are:

- CentOS 6.5 32-bit
- CentOS 6.2 32-bit and 64-bit
- CentOS 5.1 32 bit
- Microsoft® Windows® 2012 and 2012 R2
- Microsoft® Windows® 2008 and 2008 R2
- Red Hat Enterprise Linux 6.4 and 6.5 32-bit
- Red Hat Enterprise Linux AS 6.2 32-bit

As explained earlier, the Citrix Command Center also needs a database for saving information. The supported databases are:

- MSSQL 2012,2014
- MySQL 5.6
- MySQL 5.1.x with InnoDB storage engine
- Microsoft SQL Server 2005/2008/2008 R2
- Oracle Database Server 10g/11g

Supported devices

Because the Citrix Command Center can used for monitoring and managing devices, the appliances need to be supported, as follows:

- NetScaler Standard, Enterprise and Platinum edition devices, running OS versions 9.3, 10.0, 10.1, 10.5 and 11.0
- NetScaler AppFirewall
- NetScaler SDX Platform Release 9.3, 10.0, 10.1, 10.5 and 11.0
- CloudBridge
- CloudBridge Advanced Platform
- NetScaler Gateway devices, running OS versions 9.3, 10.0, 10.1, 10.5 and 11.0
- XenServer 5.6+

Hardware appliances

Citrix also provides hardware appliances for the Citrix Command Center. One of the benefits of these hardware appliances is the preloaded configuration. Also all the software and databases are installed on one appliance without imposing huge databases on production environments.

Hardware appliances are capable of managing up to 300 Citrix network appliances and have a 500 GB built-in storage.

High availability

If the Citrix Command Center is a production system and can't afford a single point of failure, then it's possible to install the Citrix Command Center in a high availability mode. The high availability mode ensures a minimum loss of functionality and there is a parallel copy of the database. When using the Citrix Command Center software, it's necessary that the database is installed on a dedicated database server that is available when one of the Citrix Command Center appliances stops running. The database will be installed in a two-way data replication mode between the primary and the secondary appliances to avoid data loss.

 The primary and secondary Citrix Command Center appliances should be configured with the same time zone or with the same time settings. This is to ensure an accurate timeline for performance data in case of a failover.

Distributed agents

To manage and monitor a large number of alliances, we can set up the Citrix Command Center in a distributed multi-tier architecture. This can be arranged by configuring Citrix Command Center agents to monitor these appliances.

When using agents, the load on the Citrix Command Center server will decrease, because the load will be divided between different agents.

When using Citrix Command Center agents in combination with the Citrix Command Center Server, the Citrix Command Center Server will perform operations, such as discovery, monitoring the appliance, configuration using configured tasks, and running processes. The agents will monitor entries and syslog messages. Also the agent will collect data such as CPU usage, resource utilization, and IP bytes transmitted for performance monitoring.

The Citrix Command Center Server and the agents are connected to the same database.

The Citrix Command Center agents can be installed after the Citrix Command Center Server is up-and-running. The installation of the agent has the same setup as the Command Center Server, except that we need to select the **Agent** option.

After installing the agent, it will be visible in the administration panel.

1. On the **Administration** tab, on the right pane, under **Tools**, click **Agent Setup**.

2. Under **Agent Details**, we can view the agent and do the following:

   ° **Name**: The IP address of the Command Center agent.

   ° **Status**: Specifies the status of the agent. The status could be: active, inactive, or has been stopped.

   ° **Action**: Based on the **Status** of an agent, we can take actions. If the agent is in an inactive state and is not managing any devices, we need to activate the agent and assign appliances to it to manage. If we want to stop an agent from managing appliances, we need to deactivate it. We can activate or deactivate an agent by selecting the agent and clicking **Activate** or **Deactivate**. To assign devices to an agent to manage, click **Assign**. If a Command Center agent is in an inactive state or has been stopped, we can unassign the appliance managed by this appliance. These appliances get assigned to the Command Center server. To unassign the devices managed by a Command Center agent, click **Unassign** for the inactive or stopped agent.

Device profiles

Device profiles contain information about the user credentials and SNMP details that are used by the Citrix Command Center to communicate with the appliance and retrieve configuration data and the SNMP traps. There are four different device profiles available for Citrix NetScaler, Citrix CloudBridge, Citrix NetScaler SDX platform, and XenServer.

Device profiles specify the user credentials and SNMP details that are used by the Command Center to communicate with the Citrix devices and retrieve configuration data and SNMP traps. You can create device profiles for the device families: NetScaler, CloudBridge, NetScaler SDX Platform. CloudBridge Advanced Platform, and XenServer. These device profiles are used by the Command Center to discover Citrix devices. Depending on the selected device, the necessary information will pop-up. This information needs to be filled to retrieve information.

Device groups

When there are multiple appliances from the same device groups, we can create device groups. These device groups can be used later for binding to a task, for example.

Port settings

The Citrix Command Center Server uses a few ports for connections. The ports that are used are listed in the following table:

Purpose	Port
HTTPS communication between Command Center client and server	TCP/8443
HTTP communication between Command Center client and server	TCP/9090
Communication between Command Center **High Availability (HA)** servers	TCP/6011, TCP/2014, and TCP/1099
SNMP communication between the Citrix Command Center server, Citrix NetScaler, and Citrix CloudBridge	TCP/161
Configuration of SNMP traps between the Command Center server and Citrix NetScaler	TCP/162
SSH and SFTP communication between the Command Center server and the Citrix NetScaler system	TCP/22
HTTPS and HTTP communication between the Command Center server and Citrix CloudBridge	TCP/443 and TCP/80
HTTPS communication between the Command Center server and NetScaler SDX	TCP/443
Communication between the Citrix Command Center server and the Citrix Command Center agents	TCP/1099
Remote Method Invocation (RMI) lookup	TCP/6011

Device discovery

Device discovery will be executed after the device was added to the Citrix Command Center. The Citrix Command Center discovers appliances based on the user credentials and/or the hostnames and IP addresses that we configured when adding the device.

After adding the device, device discovery will perform a series of steps to determine the status of the appliance. Each step and status is visible in the Citrix Command Center.

The device discovery process contains the following steps:

1. **SNMP ping**: The Citrix Command Center server sends a **Simple Network Management Protocol (SNMP)** GET request to a Citrix system-specific **object identifier** (OID). If the Citrix Command Center server successfully pings the device, it sets the status of step 2 to SUCCESS and proceeds to step 3; otherwise, the Command Center server proceeds to step 2.

2. **Find Citrix device**: The Command Center server attempts to open an SSH session to the appliance based on the device profile settings. If the SSH session fails, the device is discarded as a non-Citrix device. If the SSH session succeeds, the server issues a CLI command to check whether the device is a Citrix device. If the result is positive the Citrix Command Center will moves the appliance to the next step. Otherwise, the Citrix Command Center discards the appliance as a non-Citrix device.

3. **Enable SNMP**: On the discovered Citrix device, the Command Center executes a command to configure an SNMP community based on the details entered when configuring the map or when adding a device.

4. **Add trap destination**: The appliance communicates with the Citrix Command Center by sending trap notifications. The Citrix Command Center server adds it's IP address to the list of trap destinations on the discovered appliances. This allows the Citrix Command Center to receive all events/traps generated on the Citrix device.

5. **Collect inventory**: The Citrix Command Center server collects the basic system information for the discovered appliances using SNMP.

6. **Download files**: The Citrix Command Center server initiates a **Secure File Transfer Protocol (SFTP)** session based on the device profile. Then it downloads the configuration and license files of the device. For Citrix CloudBridge devices, it downloads only the configuration files. The Command Center server stores these files in the database.

If all the preceding steps were successfully completed, the appliance appears in the Citrix Command Center Administration page. If the Citrix Command Center Server is unable to successfully discover the appliance, it marks the device as inaccessible, generates an event, and moves the appliance to the inaccessible systems node group.

Automatic back-up

The Citrix Command Center allows inventory management. It downloads the configuration, license files, and SSL certificate from each discovered device and stores these files in the database. By default, the Citrix Command Center downloads the files during every discovery or rediscovery of a device. It's possible to download the configuration and license files in the following scenarios:

- When the Citrix Command Center receives the `save config` command
- At specific configured intervals set by the user
- During a backup operation initiated by the user

The automatic back-up functionality can be enabled through the **Administration** page.

1. On the **Administration** tab, under **Settings**, click **Inventory Settings**.
2. Select one or more of the following options for archiving:
   - **Archive "Save Config" Trap**: Select this checkbox if you want the server to archive files when the **"Save Config"** trap is received
   - **Archive Interval (in hours)**: Specify the archive interval in hours
3. In **Number of previous archive files to retain**, type the number of files that you want to retain after download.
4. Click **OK**.

Tasks

The Citrix Command Center has some tasks built-in for every device type. These tasks can be used to configure a feature in Citrix CloudBridge, for example, or to configure a Load Balancing Virtual Server on Citrix NetScaler.

Besides the built-in tasks, it's also possible to create custom tasks. These custom tasks can contain command-line code for the device. So basically full functionality can be configured with the custom tasks.

One of the advantage of tasks is the scheduling functionality. This allows us to run a task at a specific time. So for example we can create a custom task to update a Citrix NetScaler High Availability pair fully automatically. It's possible to run specific commands on Citrix NetScaler and on the Citrix Command Center itself. So uploading the firmware to Citrix NetScaler through ssh would be the first step.

Change management

When all the configuration changes of all the Citrix appliance are done through the Citrix Command Center, audit reports will be available. These audit reports display details about the type of change, the exact time of the change, and the user who made the change.

SSL certificate management

SSL certificate management enables the administrator to have central visibility and management of SSL certificates deployed on Citrix NetScaler appliances. It lists all the certificates with expiry dates. It's possible to renew certificates centrally. We can also generate signing requests (CSR) centrally and configure custom alerts based on expiry periods so that the administrator knows that a certificate will expire soon.

Reporting

The reporting feature of the Citrix Command Center enables us to monitor the performance of Citrix appliances which have been discovered, by using performance reports and threshold functionality. The Citrix Command Center monitors the health of an appliance by polling the performance counters supported by the appliance.

It's possible to generate quick reports about the performance of a specific appliance and custom reports show the performance of a set of multiple devices. We can also generate a report based on multiple counters from one or more appliances.

We can also use built-in reports and log messages to monitor security violations encountered by Citrix NetScaler Application Firewall.

Citrix NetScaler® syslog

The Citrix Command Center can also be configured to monitor Citrix NetScaler Syslog. Depending on the configuration, we can determine what type of data needs to be sent. When there is a critical error this will show up in the Citrix Command Center. The Citrix Command Center also allows us to run analytics tasks on the captured syslog messages. This allows us to search through the log files for quick analysis.

AppFirewall Signature syslog analytics

The fact that the Citrix Command Center already reads syslog message allows us also to read Application Firewall Signatures. These messages contain security violations encountered by the Application Firewall when this module is enabled in Citrix NetScaler. The built-in reports in the Citrix Command Center allow us to get a report on: top security violations, violations encountered by clients, appliances, and device profiles. We can also view the details of the Citrix NetScaler Application Firewall log.

Summary

In this chapter we described all Citrix NetScaler additional software/hardware that can be used in combination or independently.

Citrix Insight Center will give us information about the traffic flow. This can be done for HTTP traffic, ICA traffic, and for all the traffic through Citrix CloudBridge. This information contains details of WAN latency, LAN latency, jitter, compression, and so on.

Depending on the available Citrix NetScaler license, Citrix Insight Center enables us to return back in time to deliver information in the past. Web Insight doesn't require any license, and can be used as well.

Citrix CloudBridge is a appliance that can optimize traffic between two sites. Besides this, Citrix CloudBridge also supports caching for different kinds of traffic. The caching functionality allows us to send the file only once to the other side; if the file needs to be sent again, Citrix CloudBridge will send the file instead of the client/server.

Citrix CloudBridge Connector will be used to connect private datacenters to public datacenters. The CloudBridge Connector will perform the connection with IPSec or with Citrix CloudBridge's secure connection, for example. Also traffic will be optimized.

The Citrix Command Center can be used to manage and monitor different Citrix appliances. It's also possible to create custom tasks and schedule these tasks. The Citrix Command Center also performs health monitoring and will present this information on the management site. This management page can be shown on a monitor so you always get the correct status of the Citrix appliances in your network.

4
Traffic Management

NetScaler is in use in many large public organizations all over the world, doing traffic management for all of their public web services. In large organizations, you might have over 100 different services masked behind one URL with different policies and features being used. This is some of the content we will cover in this chapter:

- Content switching and policies
- DNS
- Global Server Load Balancing (GSLB)
- DataStream (SQL load balancing)
- Prioritizing with AppQoE

Content switching

Content switching is the ability to direct requests sent to the same URL to different servers with different content. Consider the scenario where, when you type the URL `http://url1.com`, you are redirected to one backend service and, if you type another URL `http://url1.com/videos`, you are redirected to another backend service even though it shares the same URL. There are also other ways besides looking at the URL to do content switching. Some examples are:

- Language
- Cookie
- IP port source/destination
- IP address source/destination
- The HTTP method POST/GET

This feature is commonly used when, for instance, delivering web services for mobile devices. If we think about accessing a website with a mobile device, we often use the same URL as we normally do but are being redirected to a mobile-friendly website on another backend resource. This is of course more user-friendly but gives us a lot of flexibility as well to split mobile traffic with regular desktop-based traffic. This also allows us to do TCP optimization based upon device connections, which will be covered in the next chapter.

In essence, content switching consists of a vServer, policies, and actions. The policies define expressions that are then evaluated to see if they trigger an action. The actions always point to a target load-balanced vServer. So let's look at this from a design perspective.

We have a website called url1.com that is accessed by two types of device: mobiles and regular computers. We therefore created a content-switching vServer that has two policies. The first policy checks if the user-agent is a mobile device; if so, it redirects the request to a vServer that is load-balancing the mobile device front-end for that service. The other policy is there to handle all other traffic, which is redirected to another load-balanced vServer that has the regular website traffic.

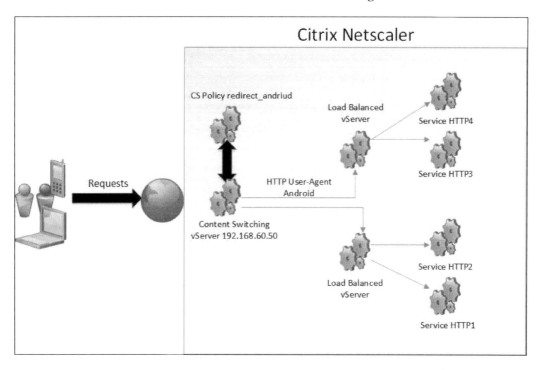

So let's set up a content switching vServer for the first scenario. First we need to enable the content switching feature; this is done by going into the management console, right-clicking on the feature, and choosing **Enable feature**.

We can also use CLI by typing the command:

```
enable feature contentswitching
```

Next we need our two load-balanced vServers in place before setting up content switching. In this scenario we just set up some vServers by using CLI.

```
Add server hostname 192.168.60.20
Add server hostname 192.168.60.21
Add server hostname 192.168.60.22
Add server hostname 192.168.60.23
```

Then we create two different services, one for mobile and another for regular HTTP traffic:

```
Add service mobile-http-1 192.168.60.20 http 80
Add service mobile-http-2 192.168.60.21 http 80
Add service http-1 192.168.60.22 http 80
Add service http-2 192.168.60.23 http 80
```

Next we need to load-balance the vServer:

```
add lb vserver HTTP-mobile-lb http 192.168.60.24 80
add lb vserver HTTP-lb http 192.168.60.25 80
```

It is important to note that we do not need to add IP addresses to the load balanced vServers if we intend to use them with content switching, since the communication between the content switching vServer and the lb vServer is only internal. In order to add a lb vServer without an IP address you need to do it using the CLI, by using the earlier example but without the IP address.

Lastly we need to bind the services to the load-balanced vServers:

```
bind lb vserver HTTP-mobile-lb mobile-http1
bind lb vserver HTTP-mobile-lb mobile-http2
bind lb vserver HTTP-lb http-1
bind lb vserver HTTP-lb http-2
```

Now that we have the load-balanced vServers in place we can create a content switching vServer:

```
Add cs vserver HTTP-CS HTTP 192.168.60.26
```

It is important to note that by default the content switching server does not check whether the backend load-balanced resources are up or not. This is because if we enable the status check this means that, for instance, if one of four load-balanced vServers is down, the content switching vServer goes down. We can enable a state check by using the command:

```
Set cs parameter -stateupdate ENABLED
```

Now we need to define the policies. Now policies, as I mentioned earlier, consist of different expressions to do an evaluation of the request. This can also be done using CLI but in this case I am going do to it using the Web GUI.

Go into **Traffic Management** | **Content Switching** and choose **Create new policy**.

There are many ways to do it this. A simple way is to create an expression that checks the user-agent string and then redirects the users to the connected backend service.

Therefore we can use the expression:

```
HTTP.REQ.HEADER("User-Agent").CONTAINS("Android")
```

Note also that instead of using expressions we can switch to using URLs; this allows us to redirect requests based upon what kind of URL the endpoint is trying to access. For instance, we can define here that a request to `http://url/resources` should be redirected to another load-balanced vServer. When we choose URL-based content switching we are also given the option to enter a domain name; this allows for NetScaler to correctly redirect content for multiple domain names.

So, all clients connecting using Android will be redirected to the server that is specified under actions.

You can find a list of the user-agent strings that can be used on this website: http://www.useragentstring.com/pages/useragentstring.php.

If we want to combine multiple expressions—for instance, a policy that binds all mobile user-agents in one expression—we can use logical operators to combine multiple expressions. We can for instance use the logical operator && that is the equivalent of AND or we can use the logical operator || that is the equivalent of OR—for instance, a compound expression containing all mobile user-agents where we want a mobile user who connects with one OR the other device redirected to a load-balanced vServer.

Now, after we have created a policy and action we have to bind it to the vServer. Go into the **Content Switching** pane. Choose **Create a new vServer**. Fill in the required information: **Name**, **Protocol**, **Port**, and **IP Address**. Click **OK**.

Under **CS Policy Binding** choose **Select policy** and add our newly created policy.

It is important to note that the priority here defines what policy runs first. If we have multiple policies with use the same expression for evaluation, the one with the lower priority wins. If you want to see how many are being redirected by the different content switching policies, you can use the following command:

```
Stat cs vserver
```

We can also use the command to see which policies are being used by the different connections:

```
nsconmsg -d current | egrep -i CSPOL
```

This allows us to see in real time which policies are triggered.

We can also define a default load balanced vServer that all other requests not caught by a policy are sent to. This is easily done by going into the content switching vServer …. **CS Policy Binding**, and choosing **Default Load Balancing Virtual Server**.

Now we have successfully created a content switching vServer that does a redirect of our users that are connecting using an Android-based device.

NOTE: it is important to know that content switching is case-sensitive by default, meaning that `http://url/A/index.html` and `http://url/a/index.html` are treated as different URLs and therefore might be redirected to different backend services. So if we want to disable the case-sensitive feature we can run this command in CLI:

```
Set cs vServer nameofvServer –casesensitive OFF
```

Another important aspect of content switching is setting up protective features. Even though content switching has monitors in place to check if the backend services are up or not, we can define a redirect URL or backup virtual server in case the CS vServer should go down or has too many connections. These settings can be defined in the vServer settings, **Protection**. Here we have a **Redirect URL** or a **Backup Virtual Server**. The redirect URL can only use HTTP or SSL because of protocol restrictions when handling redirection properly. We can also define the spillover here; spillover can be used to redirect excessive traffic to the backup vServer. It can also be specified to drop or accept excessive traffic. In order to use spillover with redirect we need to define a backup vServer and we also need to specify a threshold. For instance, let's say that our vServer can handle 10,000 connections; excessive traffic is going to be redirected to a backup vServer that is another lb vServer. If that vServer hits its limits or if both the primary vServer and the backup vServer go down, users will be redirected to the **Redirect URL**.

Protection
Redirect URL
http://nsvserver.test.local
Backup Virtual Server
testtes2 ▼
☐ Disable Primary When Down ❓

Spillover
Spillover Method*
CONNECTION ▼
Spillover Threshold
10000
Spillover Backup Action
REDIRECT ▼
Spillover Persistence Timeout (mins)
2
☑ Spillover Persistence
OK

We have also specified a **Spillover Persistence Timeout (mins)**, meaning that users that are diverted to the backup vServer have persisted connections for 2 minutes.

 Backup vServers can either be load balanced vServers or content switching vServers.

DNS

DNS is critical for all types of web applications because it allows us to use domain names—for instance www.citrix.com—instead of remembering IP addresses. It also helps SSL-based web applications with certificates to work since the trust underneath is built upon the hostname attribute or FQDN. DNS is also crucial for GSLB because it is mainly a DNS-based load-balancing feature.

NetScaler can operate as its own authoritative DNS server or use another DNS server as source and NetScaler can also serve as a proxy between authoritative DNS servers and clients.

Now by default if we add an external DNS server, the DNS communication between the NetScaler and the DNS server is sourced from the SNIP address, which is closest to the source. This means that if we have multiple SNIP addresses it will choose the closest.

To add an external DNS server we can use the following command:

```
Add nameserver ip-address –type UDP
```

 There are other options under parameter -type: UDP, TCP, or UDP_TCP. Regular DNS traffic is UDP-based but TCP is used for zone transfers for instance and for larger payloads above 512 bytes.

We also have an option here to define the nameserver as running locally; note that this is not a fully functional DNS server, since it will hand out any records (even GSLB records) without checking with the GSLB services. Features such as zone transfers are not supported in this mode, but this is the only option that works with DNS recursion. Recursion is a feature that allows NetScaler to ask other DNS servers on behalf of a querying client.

```
add dns nameserver <IP address> -local
set dns parameter -recursion ENABLED -cacheRecords YES
```

Setting up local configured entries will be synchronized to a high-availability node.

Now when we add a DNS server to NetScaler, it is added to the NS OS part of the kernel. Therefore we cannot use regular DNS-based tools such as `dig`, `nslookup` and so on to verify if the DNS server is active; this is because running these tools will only point to the local service of the DNS server. In order to verify connectivity we can use:

```
Show dns addrec FQDN
```

This will do a DNS query to the DNS server to see if the A-record is available. We can use the command:

```
Show nameserver
```

This will give us a status if the DNS server is available. Note that this is an ICMP-based monitor that is used to verify its status. So if ICMP is blocked to the DNS server the status will show as down. We can also set up NetScaler to use its own load balanced DNS server. This allows for high availability of DNS and we do not need to enable ICMP-based monitoring from the SNIP to the DNS servers. Then it will use the built-in `lb` monitor for DNS, which can be a specific DNS query (this ensures that DNS is operational and responding, not just that the host is alive).

To set up a load balanced DNS service we can just add the DNS servers as servers, add the DNS service, bind it to the backend servers, and then create a load balanced DNS vServer.

This can be done using the following command-line commands. First we add the different backend DNS servers:

```
Add server SERVERNAME 192.168.0.1
Add server SERVERNAME2 192.168.0.2
```

Then we need to create a DNS-based monitor, which is used to run a query against the different DNS servers. In this example it will query for `demo.local` and the DNS servers need to reply with the `192.168.60.1` address; if not, they will be marked as DOWN:

```
add lb monitor MONITORNAME DNS -query demo.local -queryType Address -LRTM
DISABLED -IPAddress 192.168.60.1
```

Create the service that we bind to the backend servers:

```
add service SERVICENAME SERVERNAME DNS 53
add service SERVICENAME2 SERVERNAME2 DNS 53
```

Bind the monitor to the service we created:

```
bind service SERVICENAME -monitorName MONITORNAME
bind service SERVICENAME2 -monitorName MONITORNAME
```

Then we can create a load balanced DNS vServer:

```
add lb vserver DNSLBVSERVER DNS IPaddress 53
```

Bind the services to the `lb` vServer:

```
Bind lb vserver SERVICENAME
Bind lb vserver SERVICENAME2
```

If we want traffic to the backend DNS servers to come from a specific NetScaler IP address we can use `netprofile` to assign it to a particular SNIP address.

```
Add netprofile NAMEOFPROFILE -SrcIP 192.168.60.20
Set lb DNSLBVSERVER -netprofile NAMEOFNETPROFILE
```

Note that we cannot reference a DNS server as a regular nameserver and then try to add a `lb` vServer with DNS containing the same backend server. So after we have created a load-balanced DNS vServer we can use it as a nameserver for internal name resolving for NetScaler.

```
Add nameserver NAMEOFDNSVSERVER -type UDP
```

As stated we can also use NetScaler as an authoritative DNS server. This way we can support setting up GSLB, which we will be going through later in this chapter. We can add this as a service on NetScaler by using the following command:

```
add service SERVICENAME 192.168.60.53 adns 53
```

We can check if the DNS server is working properly, just by adding an A-record to the DNS server and checking from our local client:

```
add addrec test.local 192.168.60.77
```

Then we have to do a `nslookup` from our client using the following parameters:

`nslookup test.local IPADDRESSOFDNS`

```
C:\Users\msandbu>nslookup test.local 192.168.60.53
Server:  UnKnown
Address:  192.168.60.53

Name:    test.local
Address:  192.168.60.77


C:\Users\msandbu>_
```

Global Server Load Balancing

Global Server Load Balancing (GSLB) allows us to load-balance services across different geographical regions. For instance, large organizations such as Facebook, eBay, and Microsoft use this technology to load-balance their web services. This might be for proximity reasons, because a user might be redirected to the closest available resource, or to keep redundant services available in case of datacenter failures.

So the main purposes for GSLB are:

- Performance; user proximity to the closest available resource
- Disaster recovery, where multiple sites can be grouped as primary and standby
- Load balancing resources between different multiple locations

GSLB is based upon the use of DNS. So for instance when a user wants to go to www. citrix.com, that user's DNS client will do a number of queries against the different DNS servers, until it gets a response from an authoritative source for that domain. An example might be where NetScaler, which is the authoritative nameserver for that domain, responds with an A-record to that user that is one of the load-balanced vServers attached to the domain. Before that record is handed out, NetScaler has done an evaluation of the health state of the different services the user is trying to access, using SNMP based load monitors, **Metric Exchange Protocol** (**MEP**), and explicit monitors.

GSLB also consists of different components:

- GSLB sites (that represent a geographical location or datacenter)
- GSLB services (that are linked to a load-balanced vServer)
- GSLB vServers (that consist of multiple GSLB services served from GSLB sites)

- Domains (that on NetScaler are either authoritative or act as a proxy on its behalf)
- MEP used between nodes in each site to exchange information about the state and load on the site

Before we go ahead with a design we need go a bit deeper into MEP.

MEP is a proprietary protocol used by NetScaler to communicate different GSLB site metrics, network metrics and persistence info to the other GSLB sites. Communication with MEP happens on port 3011 or 3009 for secure communication. If we want to use load-balancing methods such as proximity or RTT, we need to have MEP enabled; if not, it will fall back to round robin.

So let's look closer at an example with a small design layout.

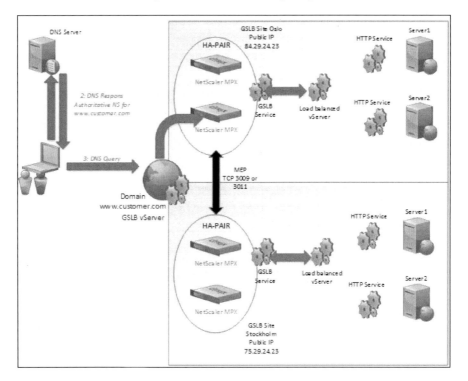

 The DNS server in this case can most likely be NetScaler, which has an ADNS service running and responding to requests.

Before we go ahead with the configuration of a GSLB site, we need to cover the first crucial part—the nameserver setup. Since the ADNS service is not highly available but running on a single NetScaler, it can become the weakest link in the event of a datacenter failure. In order to ensure high availability, we need to set up multiple ADNS services with public IPs and then add the NS records to our public domain. The way to add NS may vary from provider to provider. This is a recipe to add it on GoDaddy: `https://www.godaddy.com/help/managing-dns-for-your-domain-names-680`.

Doing this will allow clients to reference multiple nameservers and will ensure that they can connect even if one of the NetScaler pairs is down. Most DNS clients use round-robin; if one of the name servers does not respond, the DNS client will try to communicate with the next nameserver on the list.

After we have set up the nameserver configuration, we need to set up a GSLB site. A GSLB site is in most cases a representation of a datacenter or a geographical location where a network resides. We always need a local site and a remote site in a GSLB setup.

This setup will assume that we have L2 connectivity between our sites and allows us to use private IP address ranges to communicate with the different nodes in a GSLB setup.

First we need to add the local site on one of the NetScalers using the command:

```
Add gslb site NAME LOCAL IPADDRESS
```

This is shown in the following screenshot:

```
> add gslb site OSLO LOCAL 192.168.0.77
Done
>
```

Or we can add it using the GUI under **Traffic Management | GSLB | Sites** and then click on **Add**. Here we could use a SNIP or MIP address as the IP address; alternatively, in this case we used a new IP address that will represent the site. Next we need to add the remote site, using the command:

```
Add gslb site NAME REMOTE IPADDRESS
```

Here we enter the IP address of the remote NetScaler that can either be a GSLB IP or another IP that is owned by NetScaler. After we have added the two sites, we have to do the same configuration on the second NetScaler but only with opposite names and addresses. After this is done we can verify that we have completed the setup correctly and that MEP is active, using the command:

`Show gslb site`

After this is done we need to add services to the individual sites; these are typical services that serve the same content (for example, web servers and so on) and are typically represented as a load balanced vServer or a content-switching vServer.

We can start by adding a GSLB service to one of the NetScalers using the GUI; this will be one of the existing load balanced vServers on the NetScaler that represents some web servers.

Now when adding the service, we have some different options (for instance if we want to add a virtual server), as shown in the following screenshot:

That site we want to set up the service, what service type and so on. When we click **Add** we are given more options such as:

- Monitors
- Monitor threshold
- DNS views
- Site persistence
- Other settings

The important part here is monitors. Monitors can be configured if we want explicit monitors attached to the load balancing vServer; by default, MEP will control the health status of the service. If we configure a monitor it will then override MEP for health monitoring. If we, for instance, do not have the option to use MEP, we should use monitors against remote services. After we are done with adding the service, we also have to add the service on the remote site, using the same wizard but instead choosing the other site. When we choose the other, remote, site, we are not given the option to choose a virtual server and therefore need to choose from existing servers.

After we have added the necessary services to the first site, we need to add them to the second site as well; just remember that we have to adjust the site location and IP addresses.

When we have added services to both sites and the MEP is communicating, we can see that the status and health information will be exchanged.

This can be seen by using the command:

```
Show gslb service SERVICENAME or stat GSLB SERVICENAME
```

Now that we have added the services on both of the sites we have to create a GSLB virtual server.

This can be done by using the command:

```
Add gslb vserver VSERVERNAME
```

Or by using GUI **Traffic Management | GSLB | Virtual Servers**. Give the vServer a name. It is important to note that not all options are available before we click **OK**.

By default the vServer is set to serve A-records when a client requests something and the service type is HTTP; this just defines what type of services we are able to add to the vServer.

After creating the vServer we have the option to bind services to it, under the **Service** menu option, the result of which is shown in the following screenshot:

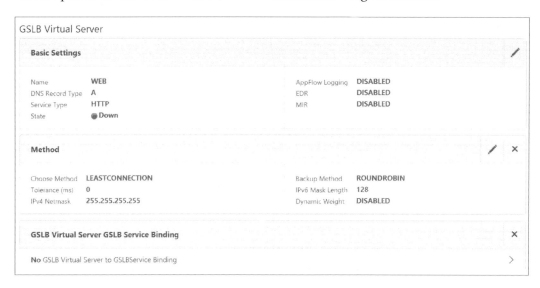

When we are done adding services to the vServer we should configure the load balancing methods (the default is LEASTCONNECTIONS).

Load balancing methods

There are multiple methods that we can use for load balancing:

- LEASTCONNECTIONS
- ROUNDROBIN
- LEASTRESPONSETIME
- SOURCEIPHASH
- LEASTBANDWIDTH
- LEASTPACKETS
- STATICPROXIMITY
- RTT

There are two options here that are specific for GSLB: STATICPROXIMITY and RTT. STATICPROXIMITY can use a custom location database to determine where to send clients, or we create our own custom entries.

In order to use a location database, we have to buy one from commercially configured third-party databases such as **maxmind.com** (`https://www.maxmind.com/en/home`), for instance.

In order to use custom entries, we just have to add an IP-range and set a location qualifier. By default NetScaler uses the following qualifiers for a location database:

```
continent.country.region.city.isp.organization
```

For instance if we have an IP-range that we know is in Norway we could add the following custom entries:

Add location 192.168.0.0 192.168.0.255

EU.NO.AKERHUS.OSLO.TELENOR.CITRIX

Now, after we have added the location, we have to set NetScaler to use the location parameter. So let's say that we want traffic coming from that particular IP address range to communicate with a particular NetScaler; we need to set the location parameter to use one of the qualifiers that we entered. This can be done using one of the six different qualifiers.

For instance:

set locationparameter -context custom -q2label NO

-q2label determines what qualifier to use. If we want to base it upon a continent, we need to change the command to -q1label; if we want to base it upon an organization, we need to set it to -q6label and so on.

This will set up NetScaler to use a static, proximity-based decision and all addresses coming from within that range will get a response from the one with the location parameter set. If an IP address outside that range tries to communicate, NetScaler will fall back to round-robin-based load balancing.

RTT is a dynamic proximity load balancing method that measures the delay between a client's local DNS server and the data resource it is trying to access. After it has measured the RTT, NetScaler then exchanges the metric with the other sites using MEP and then sorts out the RTT between the different sites and the client. Then it makes its load balancing decision and will dynamically redirect the client request to the GSLB site that has the lowest RTT. NetScaler uses different probes to determine the RTT. By default it uses PING first; if that fails it tries a DNS UDP probe. If that does not work it tries a DNS TCP probe.

If all probes fail or RTT metrics are not available, NetScaler will fall back to round-robin load-balancing.

If we want to change the order of the probes we can do so using the following command:

```
set gslb parameter -ldnsprobeOrder DNS PING TCP
```

This might be necessary for instance if we do not allow external PING traffic via the firewall or UDP.

After we have configured the load balancing method we have to add a domain to the vServer. That can be done under the domain pane in the vServer options.

When we add the domain name, NetScaler will automatically create an A-record for it under DNS records. This will then be used by the ADNS service to respond with the domain name to clients.

Now after we have added a domain to the virtual server, we can verify that the services are up by using the command:

```
Show gslb domain test.local
```

We can also verify that the address record is set to a GSLB site by using the command:

```
Show addrec test.local
```

It is important that we also create the virtual server on the second site and add the same domain name, or else MEP might not work properly. As it might be cumbersome to do the same configuration on multiple NetScalers, Citrix has created a `Sync` option to sync configuration between a master NetScaler and other remote sites. This can be done using the command:

```
Sync gslb config
```

It is important to note that this option uses SSH to communicate and therefore if we have a dedicated site IP setup we need to enable that IP to use SSH, which is not enabled by default on GSLB IPs or SNIP addresses. This can be done in the GUI under **System | Network | IPs**. Choosing the GSLB site IP, **Edit**, choosing enable management access and adding SSH.

The option will also initiate from the NSIP from the master NetScaler (the one we initiate the synchronization from).

After the synchronization is done, we can verify the status by using the command:

```
Show gslb syncstatus
```

Now that this is done we can verify it by setting our client IP address DNS server to use the NetScaler ADNS IP. Then we can use `nslookup`, as shown in the following screenshot, to verify that the records we get are the virtual services in the GSLB setup.

```
C:\Users\msandbu>nslookup test.local
Server:  UnKnown
Address:  192.168.0.71

Name:     test.local
Address:  192.168.0.70

C:\Users\msandbu>nslookup test.local
Server:  UnKnown
Address:  192.168.0.71

Name:     test.local
Address:  10.0.0.1
```

Since my GSLB site setup is based upon round-robin I will get both of the records. If I set the persistence to static proximity and use the location parameter, I will be redirected to the one that has the closest qualifier set.

This setup used an active/active GSLB configuration, which means that traffic would be distributed between both sites. In some cases, we might also use an active/passive setup for disaster recovery purposes.

Active/passive GSLB

In order to set up an active/passive GSLB configuration, we first need to set up a GSLB site configuration

First we need to add the two sites that will act as active/passive, by using the following CLI commands:

```
add gslb site sitePRI LOCAL 192.168.0.200 -publicIP 192.168.0.200
add gslb site siteSEC REMOTE 192.168.0.100 -publicIP 192.168.0.100
```

Then we run the following command to add a vServer to the GSLB site located on the primary site:

```
add gslb vserver RPIserver http -lbmethod RTT
```

Now we need to add a service that will serve content from the primary site:

```
add service serverPRI 192.168.0.201
add lb vserver vserverPRI HTTP 192.168.0.202 80
bind lb vserver vserverPRI serverPRI
```

Now that we have a load-balanced vServer we need to bind this as a GSLB service and then attach it to the GSLB vServer on the primary site:

```
add gslb service gslb-srv-PRI 192.168.0.202 HTTP 80 -sitename sitePRI
bind gslb vserver PRIserver -servicename gslb-srv-PRI
```

And then lastly we attach a domain name to that particular vServer:

```
bind gslb vserver vserverPRI -domainname www.test.com
```

Now that we have successfully created the primary GSLB site and have configured it to have a GSLB service and respond to a domain name, we have to configure it to have a secondary site as backup. First we need to add a new GSLB vServer:

```
add gslb vserver SECserver HTTP
```

Then we need to attach a service to that GSLB vServer:

```
add gslb service gslb-srv-SEC 192.168.0.101
bind gslb vserver SECserver -serviceName gslb-srv-SEC
```

Then lastly we need to configure the backup parameter on the primary VServer:

```
set GSLB vserver PRIserver -backupVServer SECserver
```

Now we need to repeat the configuration on the secondary site; if we do not do this the information exchange will not happen and requests might fail if the primary goes down.

First we need to add the sites:

```
add gslb site sitePRI REMOTE 192.168.0.200 -publicIP 192.168.0.200
add gslb site siteSEC LOCAL 192.168.0.100 -publicIP 192.168.0.100
```

Next add a GSLB vServer that will act as the backup for the primary on the other site:

```
add gslb vserver SECserver http -lbmethod RTT
```

Now we need to add a local service on the NetScaler and then bind it to a load balanced vServer:

```
add service serverSEC 192.168.0.101
add lb vserver vserverSEC HTTP 80
bind lb vserver vserverSEC serverSEC
```

Now that we have created the load-balanced vServer we need to create it as a GSLB service:

```
add gslb service gslb-srv-SEC 192.168.0.101 HTTP 80 -sitename siteSEC
bind gslv vserver SECserver -servicename gslb-srv-SEC
```

And now we need to add the GSLB vServer on the primary site so we can reference it:

```
add gslb vserver PRIserver HTTP
```

Then we attach a service to it:

```
add gslb service gslb-srv-PRI 192.168.0.201
bind gslb vserver PRIserver -servicename gslb-srv-PRI
```

Now we need to bind a domain name to the GSLB vServer on the primary site:

```
bind gslb vserver PRIserver -domainname www.test.com
```

Lastly we configure the secondary vServer to act as a backup for the primary:

```
set GSLB vserver PRIserver -backupVServer SECserver
```

Troubleshooting GSLB

GSLB is a complex feature that might often lead to headaches if not properly configured. Therefore, it is crucial to know where to start if we need to troubleshoot a configuration.

 A good way to start is to look at the domains configured in the GSLB setup and look at the visualizer; this will give you a graphical overview of how the configuration is for that particular domain name.

Some basics to check for if GSLB is not working or if we cannot perform the configuration:

- Do we have the correct license?

  Use the show license command in the CLI to see if GSLB is available. If it isn't, we need to upgrade to Enterprise or buy it as an add-on feature in Standard.

- Is the feature enabled?

  Use the show feature command in CLI to see if the GSLB feature is enabled or not. If it isn't, we can use the enable feature GSLB command to enable the feature.

- Is DNS working as it should?

  Can clients resolve the IP address of the GSLB services? In some cases we should enable the vServer to return the IP addresses of all the services to make sure that it returns the correct IP addresses. This can be done by changing the configuration on the GSLB vServer using CLI:

  ```
  Set gslb vserver VSERVERNAME -MIR ENABLED
  ```

- Are the nameserver and start of authority records added to the domain records or at the domain registrar?

- The best way to check this is by using nslookup on a client. Start cmd, type nslookup, where the client is preferably configured with a public DNS server, then type:

  ```
  Set type=NS
  Domainname.example
  ```

  This should return the authoritative DNS servers for the domain that is configured to be used with GSLB — for instance, the ADNS service running on the NetScalers.

- Is the NetScaler setup an ADNS or is it a proxy for an internal DNS server?

  If the NetScaler is to act as an authoritative DNS server it needs to have the ADNS service running and be listed as the NS record for the public domain. If it is to act a proxy DNS server, we need to add the internal DNS server as a vServer.

  ```
  Add service DNS_SVC1 192.168.0.101 DNS 53
  Add lb vserver DNS_VSERV1 DNS 192.168.0.102 53
  Bind lb vserver DNS_VSERV1 DNS_SVC1
  ```

- Is the configuration correct on all participating nodes?

  Use the command `show gslb runningConfig` to see if the configuration is configured properly.

- Is proximity load balancing not working?

  Make sure that the load balancing method is properly set on all participating nodes, and, if that a static proximity location is being set, that the location qualifier is set properly. This can be checked by specifying a custom IP range and connecting using a client from that range. If RTT dynamic proximity is being used, make sure that the probes work as intended; for instance, if the firewall is blocking DNS or ICMP requests, it might cause the probes to fail.

- Is MEP not working?

  Make sure that the ports needed for MEP are open between the site IP addresses.

- Is traffic not being load balanced correctly?

- Are some clients unable to resolve the correct IP addresses?

DataStream

The DataStream feature provides us with an intelligent mechanism for load balancing SQL traffic to backend endpoints. This might for instance be based upon READ and WRITE requests, where READ requests are forwarded to some dedicated backend SQL servers while WRITE requests are dedicated to a master cluster.

This can also be performed down to a database level, where we can load-balance specific databases, or can even be based upon other attributes such as usernames, packet size, and so on.

 The DataStream feature is only supported for MySQL and MS SQL databases.

For MySQL, DataStream supports versions 4.1, 5, 5.1, 5.4, 5.5, and 5.6 using native MySQL authentication. For MS SQL it supports 2005, 2008, 2008 R2, 2012, and 2014 (only frontend) using both SQL authentication and NTLM or Kerberos using the TDS protocol.

This book will only focus on SQL authentication against MS SQL.

Setting up generic SQL load balancing

In order to set up the DataStream feature, there are some prerequisites that need to be in place first.

First we need a database user in place. This is a user that the NetScaler uses to connect to the backend servers. For instance, to use with a monitor to verify that the database is working, NetScaler also uses the database user to authenticate the clients, which are then redirected to the backend servers.

In order to set up a database user, go into **System | User Administration | Database User**, and enter a username and password for a database user. It is important to note that usernames are case-sensitive. If you update the password for the SQL user in MS SQL, you will also need to update the database user on NetScaler.

Next we should configure a database profile, this profile is used with for instance setting up different editions of MS SQL served as a frontend.

Now we need to create a MS SQL monitor; this can be done under **Traffic Management | Load Balancing | Monitors**, then click **Add**. From here choose type MSSQL-ECV, then go into special parameters. Here we need to type the username of the database user we created earlier. It is important that this user has database reader access to the particular database we want to test against, because it is used to run a SQL query against a database to ensure that the database is operational.

Next type the name of the database we want to monitor against, then type a query that is then used against that particular database. This might for instance be a select statement such as SELECT * FROM TABLE. Then under expression we need to enter an expression that defines how NetScaler will verify whether the SQL server is up or not. In our example, it is MSSQL.RES.ATLEAST_ROWS_COUNT(0), which means that, when NetScaler runs the query against the database, it should return zero rows from that particular table.

There are also some other parameters that we can define here, such as:

- **Protocol version**: Defines the backend SQL server version that is running
- **KCD account**: If we are using Windows-based authentication, we can define a Kerberos constrained delegation account that can be used to access the databases
- **Store DB**: This feature is used to store all databases retrieved from the backend database servers, in specific database load balancing

Now, after we have created an MSSQL monitor, we can set up a load balanced SQL deployment by creating a vServer and attaching the needed backend services. When setting up the load-balanced vServer it is important to remember to select MSSQL as the protocol and that the port number is set to 1433 as a default by MSSQL.

We can use NetScaler to proxy against different versions of MSSQL; even if the backend servers are version 2014, we can specify that the virtual server should represent itself as a 2012 vServer for compatibility.

This is done under the **MsSql** pane by choosing the **Server Version**, as shown in the following screenshot:

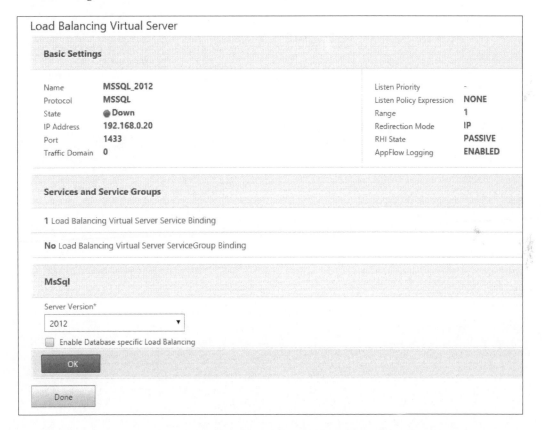

It is also here that we define whether we want to have database-specific load balancing, which will be covered a bit later in this chapter.

Master/slave deployment

This deployment uses an optional content-switching vServer to be able to load balance reads and writes between different backend virtual servers.

Here we use a content switch policy to forward SELECT statements to some servers and redirect WRITE requests to a master server.

This is shown in the following diagram:

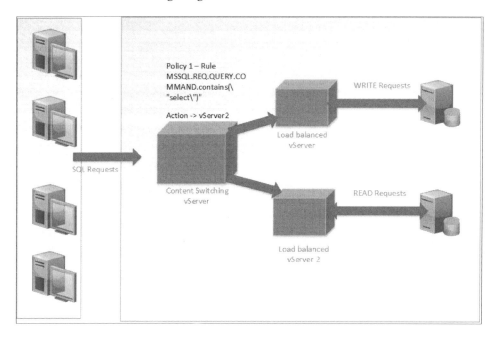

Here we have a simple action policy attached to the content switching vServer that redirects select statements to a particular slave server for read requests. All other requests are sent to the master server that in most cases are WRITE requests.

In order to set this up we need to predefine the load balancing vServers and then create a content-switching vServer. Go into **Traffic Management | Content Switching | Virtual Servers** then click on **Add**. Enter the necessary info and be sure to choose the MSSQL protocol and port 1433 (in the case of MSSQL).

We also have the same options on the content switching VServer to define MSSQL server versions.

Next we need to create a **Content Switching Policy,** and click on the **+** sign to create a new policy. Under the **Expression** tab write MSSQL.REQ.QUERY.COMMAND. contains("select").

Then we need to define an action for if someone matches the expression. By the **Action** pane click the **+** sign; then, under **target load balancing virtual server**, choose the virtual server that represents the servers handling READ requests.

When adding the policy to the vServer, give it a low priority. This is because then the content-switching vServer will evaluate requests first by checking against the expression; if it does not fulfill the statement, it will be sent to the other server.

Next we just need to define a default load balancing virtual server that will be the one that represents the master servers (WRITE requests).

AppQoE

AppQoE is a combination of different features on NetScaler—more precisely, HTTPDoS, priority queuing, and SureConnect.

This feature allows us to prioritize traffic based upon different parameters—for instance, where the endpoint is coming from or what kind of endpoint is connecting with the use of expressions. So, for instance, let's say we have an e-commerce website that serves both mobile and desktop users. From experience, we see that desktop devices are more likely to buy something from the site than mobile devices. In that case, if the e-commerce site reaches its maximum threshold or bandwidth, we need to prioritize the traffic and then we want desktop users to get access before mobile users.

To configure AppQoE, we need to define a policy that contains an expression and an action. For instance, this might be an expression containing Android devices:

```
HTTP.REQ.HEADER("User-Agent").CONTAINS("Android")
```

That will then have an action attached to it; the action might be what to do with the traffic that matches the expression. This might for instance be to prioritize the traffic, or to display a custom wait page, and so on.

In order to set up AppQoE, we first need to enable the feature either using CLI:

```
Enable feature appqoe
```

Or using the management interface, by going into **AppExpert** | **AppQoE**, right-clicking and choosing **Enable feature**.

Then we start by creating an action, by going into the **Actions** pane and clicking **Add**.

So let's create an action that will apply to Android devices.

Here there are some actions that can be set:

- **Action Type**
  - ° ACS
  - ° NS
  - ° No action

- **Priority**
- **Policy Queue Depth**
- **Queue Depth**
- **DOS Action**

Action Type defines what action to take when the threshold is reached. There are three types of action we can take. **Alternative Content Service (ACS)** can be used to redirect requests to another vServer on the NetScaler. For instance, the following screenshot shows an action that will allow NetScaler to serve alternate content, using a custom path, and that will be displayed only if it matches the thresholds, which can either be based upon max connections or delay:

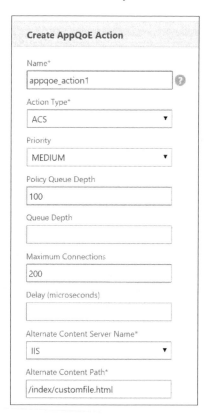

We also have the NS option under **Action Type**; this allows us to, for instance, display a custom HTML page to end users trying to connect to the vServer. In order to choose a custom HTML page, we must first upload one to the NetScaler under **AppExpert | AppQoE | HTML Page Imports** and by choosing **Add**.

We also have the option to not set an action type; this will not allow NetScaler to display any custom content and any connections that are over the threshold will be placed in the lowest priority queue.

Priority defines what priority the traffic should have. There are four values to choose from here: HIGH, MEDIUM, LOW, LOWEST. Traffic will always be processed in that order.

As an example we could have a policy aimed at mobile users, where we have defined all mobile traffic with the priority set to MEDIUM by default, and another policy with priority set to HIGH for desktop users. This would mean that all desktop user traffic would be processed first and mobile traffic would be processed afterwards.

 When no priority is set, NetScaler will fall back to the lowest priority.

Policy Queue Depth is a value we define on how many connections fall within this policy. Subsequent connections are assigned to the LOWEST priority rights.

Queue Depth is a value that defines how many connections fall within this policy on this particular priority; subsequent connections are assigned to the LOWEST priority rights.

Maximum Connections defines how many concurrent connections can be active before NetScaler triggers an action; likewise, delay is defined in microseconds before NetScaler triggers an action.

Lastly we have **DOS Action**, which is in essence the HTTPDoS feature; this feature will be covered in much greater detail. In order to define a HTTPDoS action within AppQoE, we just have to define an expression that might be filtering on an HTTP user agent and define an action type that can be SimpleResponse and HICresponse.

It is important to note that we do not define a value for when the DOS action will trigger; this is done globally for AppQoE, and can be configured under **AppExpert | AppQoE | Configure AppQoE parameters | DOS Attack threshold**. Here we can define the average number of client connections that can queue up before the DOS action triggers.

After we have created an action, we have to bind it to a policy. Policies need to contain an expression that can be using HTTP user agents, IP source, and so on.

After we have created the policy we need to bind it to a vServer. This can be done by going into a particular vServer, **Policies** | **Choose Policy** | **AppQoE**, then binding the policy that we created.

 We can look at the statistics for an AppQoE policy by using the CLI command:

`Stat appqoe policy policyname`

Summary

In this chapter, we explored different traffic management features, such as content switching, GSLB, and DataStream. We also took a closer look at AppQoE and how we can use it to prioritize traffic when needed.

In the next chapter, we will take a closer look at how we can fine-tune NetScaler using different TCP and other networking features. We will also examine in greater detail how we can monitor the NetScaler appliance using built-in features and Citrix products such as Insight and TaaS.

5

Tuning and Monitoring NetScaler® Performances

Since NetScaler plays a central role in delivering backend services to users, it is important that we can properly optimize the traffic going back and forth depending on endpoints, what kind of connection they have, and the bridge between virtual/ physical networks. In this chapter, we will look more closely at:

- Tuning the network and virtual environment
- TCP and SSL profiles
- Monitoring network traffic
- Monitoring NetScaler performance

Tuning the network and virtual environment

If we are deploying a NetScaler in a virtual environment it is crucial that we have properly configured the virtual appliance. For instance, it is important that we do not over-allocate vCPU in a virtual environment, since NetScaler mostly uses the CPU to handle all of the network traffic such as SSL traffic, content switching, and so on.

Also it is important that we configure the appliance itself to be placed on a virtual environment that either has cluster functionality or on which we have implemented high-availability such as active/passive or even NetScaler clustering.

We should also have some form of NIC teaming on the host level so that, in the event of NIC failure, the network traffic can still be served.

It is also important that, if we implement host level NIC teaming, we understand how the various types of NIC teaming perform traffic processing. For instance, Microsoft Hyper-V has a form of NIC teaming called switch independent mode that allows us to connect a physical host to different switches and does not require us to do any form of configuration on the switches. However, this means that only one NIC can receive traffic at a time.

This might be an issue for NetScaler, which—in some cases such as ICA traffic—requires that the traffic originates from one source MAC.

Most vendors have good documentation on their NIC teaming features. For example, Microsoft has documented all the different options here:

`http://www.microsoft.com/en-us/download/details.aspx?id=30160`.

But if NIC teaming is required it should be set up using LACP or LAG, which allows for aggregation of bandwidth (incoming/outgoing) and redundancy of NICs.

Note also that features such as SR-IOV and PCI device pass-through are not supported for NetScaler VPX.

As I mentioned with regard to CPUs, it is important that we configure the amount of vCPU based upon the VPX model we have. NetScaler uses something called packet engines. In a basic setup with two vCPUs, the first CPU is used for management purposes and the second vCPU is used to process all network packets.

VPX 10 and 200 only support having one packet engine CPU, meaning a total of two vCPUs, while for instance VPX 1000 supports having two or three packet engine vCPUs. This allows NetScaler to distribute traffic between the different vCPUs and will allow for better performance that the following chart shows the different editions and support for multiple packet engines.

License/memory	2 GB	4 GB	6 GB	8 GB	10 GB	12 GB
VPX 10	1	1	1	1	1	1
VPX 200	1	1	1	1	1	1
VPX 1000	1	2	3	3	3	3
VPX 3000	1	2	3	3	3	3

This feature is available for KVM, XenServer, VMware, and Hyper-V.

If you are running an older version of Hyper-V, this feature might not be supported. To ensure compatibility, you should upgrade to a later version of NetScaler.

It is important to remember that, when we are monitoring the CPU metric at a hypervisor level on NetScaler, it might give false alarms. Since the CPU in NetScaler is always looking for work even if there is nothing to do, it will always look like it is fully utilized.

 Proper CPU usage can be seen using the CLI command `stat system`.

In order to get proper reporting on the CPU usage on a NetScaler appliance, it can be viewed from the NetScaler dashboard itself, CLI, or (for instance) by using Citrix NetScaler Insight.

If we have an SNMP-enabled monitoring system, we can also configure alarms in order to get alerts if a CPU is above a certain point.

There are three CPU-based alerts, which are by default not enabled:

- `MGMT-CPU-USAGE`
- `CPU-USAGE`
- `AVERAGE-CPU`

With NetScaler 11, Citrix introduced support for jumbo frames for VPX. This allows for a much higher payload in an Ethernet frame. Instead of the traditional 1,500 bytes we can scale up to 9,000 bytes of payload. This allows for much lower overhead since the frames contain more data.

This requires that the underlying NIC on the hypervisor support this feature and that it is enabled as well. NetScaler can proxy jumbo frame connections; this means that traffic originating from ports that do not support jumbo frames but use the standard 1,500 MTU can be proxied to NetScaler and then be sent across to backend resources using jumbo frames.

This is typically the case if we have clients originating from the Internet, since most ISPs, firewalls, and routers only process packets that use the standard packet size; then NetScaler can optimize the traffic going to the backend resources by using jumbo frame connectivity.

This feature is configured on an interface level, so in most cases this feature can only be used in a two-arm NIC deployment. Using one-arm mode with jumbo frames is not going to work properly.

To configure it we need to go to **System | Network | Interface**, select an interface and click **Edit**. Here we have the option called **Maximum Transmission Unit** that can be adjusted up to 9,216 bytes.

Most hypervisors also make use of something called VMQ (Hyper-V), NetQueue (VMware), which allows the physical NIC to queue traffic to a specific core on the hypervisor. If this feature is not enabled, all inbound traffic on the hypervisor is processed on a single core (that can handle about 3.5 Gbps).

TCP and SSL profiles

Since most of the traffic going through the Internet today is based upon TCP, it is important that it is properly configured. Since endpoints might come from many different locations—such as a PC connected to a fast Ethernet connection or a mobile device using 3G/4G—the connection needs to behave differently.

TCP has many different parameters that by default on NetScaler are not configured. This is because NetScaler is configured to fit into most environments, and even though many of the TCP options might give a performance boost they might also degrade performance if not properly configured.

This is where TCP profiles come in. TCP profiles allow us to configure a set of different TCP settings into a profile that we can then attach to a virtual server or a set of services. For instance, TCP traffic should behave differently for mobile devices browsing a mobile website located on a load-balanced vServer than for traffic going to backend resources connected on a fast Ethernet LAN.

Citrix has created a lot of built-in TCP profiles that are custom made for different types of connection and service. By default, NetScaler uses a built-in profile called `nstcp_default_profile`; the profile can be seen under **System | Profiles | TCP Profiles**.

This default profile has most of the different TCP features turned off, to ensure compatibility with most infrastructures. The profile has not been adjusted much since it was first added in NetScaler.

We also have other TCP profiles that are suited for particular services, such as `nstcp_default_XA_XD_profile`, which is intended for ICA-proxy traffic and has some differences from the default profile such as:

- **Window Scaling**
- **Selective Acknowledgement**
- **Forward Acknowledgement**
- **Use Nagle's algorithm**

Window Scaling is a TCP option that allows the receiving point to accept more data than allowed in the TCP RFC for window size before getting an acknowledgement. By default, the window size is set to accept 65,536 bytes. With **Window Scaling** enabled, it basically bitwise-shifts the window size. This is an option that needs to be enabled on both endpoints in order to be used, and will only be sent in the initial three way handshake.

Selective Acknowledgement (SACK) is a TCP option that allows for better handling of TCP retransmission. In the scenario where two hosts communicate with SACK not enabled and suddenly one of the hosts drops out of the network and loses some packets, when it comes back online it receives more packets from the other host. In this case the first host will ACK from the last packet it got from the other host before it dropped out. With SACK enabled, it will notify the other host of the last packet it got before it dropped out, and the other packets it received when it got back online. This allows for faster communication recovery since the other host does not need to resend all the packets.

Forward Acknowledgement (FACK) is a TCP option that works in conjunction with SACK and helps avoid TCP congestion by measuring the total number of data bytes outstanding in the network. Using the information from SACK it can more precisely calculate how much data it can retransmit.

Nagle's algorithm is a TCP feature that tries to cope with small packet problems. Applications such as Telnet often send each keystroke within its own packet, creating multiple small packets containing only 1 byte of data, which results in a 41-byte packet for one keystroke. The algorithm works by combining a number of small outgoing messages into the same message, thus avoiding overhead.

ICA is a protocol that operates by sending many small packets, which might create congestion on the network; this is why Nagle is enabled in the TCP profile. Also since many might be connecting using 3G or Wi-Fi, which might in some cases be unreliable when it comes to changing channel, we need options that require the clients to be able to reestablish a connection quickly and that allow the use of SACK and FACK.

Note that Nagle might have negative performance on applications that have their own buffering mechanism and operate inside the LAN.

Since ICA-proxy mostly uses TCP, except for Framehawk traffic using DTLS, this should be enabled for NetScaler Gateway vServers.

If we take a look at another profile such as `nstcp_default_lan`, we can see that FACK is disabled; this is because the resources needed to calculate the amount of outstanding data in a high-speed network might be too much for the CPU to handle.

So let's go into some of the other different TCP parameters in slightly greater depth:

- **Maximum Burst Limit**: This setting controls the burst of TCP segments on the wire in a single attempt. A higher limit here ensures faster delivery of data in a congestion-free network. Limiting bursts of packets helps to avoid congestion.

- **Initial Congestion Window size**: Initial congestion window defines the number of bytes that can be outstanding in the beginning of a transaction. The default size is 4 (that is 4*MSS).

- **TCP Delayed ACK Time-out (msec)**: To minimize the number of ACK packets on the wire, this NetScaler feature by default sends ACK only to a sending node if the NetScaler receives two data packets consecutively or the timer expires; the default timeout is 200 ms.

- **Maximum ooo packet queue size**: This feature allows out-of-order packets in TCP streams to be cached in system memory and reassembled before they are processed by NetScaler. By default the value is 64; we can define a value of 0 that means no limit but this will put a lot of strain on the NetScaler memory usage.

- **MSS** and **Maximum Packets per MSS**: With this setting we can specify the maximum segment size to be used for TCP transactions. It is important to note that jumbo frames will override this setting, since MSS is TCP sizes and MTU is IP packets, which is lower in the network layer. So if we specify a higher MTU size on the interface by enabling jumbo frames the MSS size will increase as well.

- **Maximum Packets Per Retransmission**: This setting controls how many packets are retransmitted in a single attempt. This is used with TCP Reno that used a partial ACK value to notify NetScaler that is has received some of the packets but not all.

- **TCP Buffer Size (bytes)**: The buffer size is the receiver buffer size on the NetScaler. The buffer size is advertised to clients and servers from NetScaler and it controls their ability to send data to NetScaler. The default size is 8K and in most cases it will be beneficial to increment this when communicating with internal server farms.

Another important aspect of these profiles is the TCP congestion algorithms. For instance, `nstcp_default_mobile` uses the Westwood congestion algorithm, because it is much better at handling large bandwidth-delay paths such as wireless.

The following congestion algorithms are available in NetScaler:

- Default (based upon TCP Reno)
- Westwood (based upon TCP Westwood+)
- BIC
- CUBIC
- Nile (based upon TCP-Illinois)

What is worth noting here is that Westwood is aimed at 3G/4G connections, or other slow wireless connections. BIC is aimed at high-bandwidth connections with high latency, such as WAN connections. CUBIC is almost like BIC but not as aggressive when it comes to fast-ramp and retransmissions. It is important to note however that CUBIC is the default TCP algorithm in Linux kernels from 2.6.19 to 3.1.

Nile is a new algorithm created by Citrix and was introduced in NetScaler 11, which is based upon TCP-Illinois. This is targeted at high-speed, long-distance networks. It achieves higher throughput than standard TCP and is also compatible with standard TCP.

There are also some other parameters that are important to think about in the TCP profile.

One of these parameters is Multipath TCP. This feature permits endpoints that have multiple paths to a service, typically a mobile device that has WLAN and 3G capabilities, and allows the device to communicate with a service on a NetScaler using both channels at the same time. This requires that the device support communication on both methods and that the service or application on the device support **Multipath TCP (MPTCP)**.

As I mentioned, NetScaler includes a range of different profiles that are aimed at different connections. Here is a summary of the different TCP profiles and where they should be used:

- `nstcp_default_tcp_lfp`: This profile is useful for long fat pipe networks (WAN) on the client side. Long fat pipe networks have long delay, high bandwidth lines with minimal packet drops.

- `nstcp_default_tcp_lnp`: This profile is useful for long narrow pipe networks (WAN) on the client side. Long narrow pipe networks have considerable packet loss once in a while.

- `nstcp_default_tcp_lan`: This profile is useful for backend server connections, where these servers reside on the same LAN as a NetScaler appliance.

- `nstcp_default_tcp_lfp_thin_stream`: This profile is similar to the `nstcp_default_tcp_lfp` profile. However, the settings are tuned for small packet flows.

- `nstcp_default_tcp_lnp_thin_stream`: This profile is similar to the `nstcp_default_tcp_lnp` profile. However, the settings are tuned for small packet flows.

- `nstcp_default_tcp_lan_thin_stream`: This profile is similar to the `nstcp_default_tcp_lan` profile. However, the settings are tuned to small packet flows.

- `nstcp_default_tcp_interactive_stream`: This profile is similar to the `nstcp_default_tcp_lan` profile. However, it has a reduced delayed ACK timer and ACK on PUSH packet settings.

- `nstcp_internal_apps`: This profile is useful for internal applications on a NetScaler appliance. This contains tuned window scaling and SACK options for the required applications. This profile should not be bound to applications other than internal applications.

Note that TCP profiles can be attached to a service, for backend communication, and to a vServer that communicates with the different client endpoints. In order to add a TCP profile just go into a service or vServer, go into the **Profiles** pane, and choose a TCP profile from the list.

 AOL has a presentation on what it optimized in its environment when setting up NetScaler. You can view it here: `http://www.slideshare.net/masonke/net-scaler-tcpperformancetuningintheaolnetwork`.

We also have SSL profiles that define how SSL traffic should be processed on a NetScaler. With SSL it means that we can define that cipher groups can be used and how and when NetScaler should encrypt data. The common issue with SSL traffic is that the more advanced the encryption we choose, the less performance we get; this is because it requires more compute capabilities to encrypt data using more advanced algorithms such as AES instead of, for instance, RC4.

When creating SSL profiles, we need to define if they are going to be frontend or backend. Frontend SSL profiles can only be attached to virtual servers, while backend ones can only be attached to services.

[Not all parameters are available when configuring a backend SSL profile.]

There are a few parameters that we should be aware of when configuring SSL profiles:

- **Quantum size**
- **PUSH Encryption Trigger**
- **Protocols**
- **Enable DH Param**

The **Quantum size** defines how much data in KB should be processed before it is encrypted. By default, this value is 8,192 KB; if we are hosting a service that provides media downloads, for instance, or large files in general, we will get a benefit if we change this to a larger quantum size.

By default, the **PUSH Encryption Trigger** value is used to tell NetScaler how long it should wait before consolidating the data and encrypting it.

For instance, ICA-proxy sessions have the PSH flag set, which means that NetScaler should always forward encrypted traffic without delay; if we set this value to 5ms, NetScaler will gather data for 5ms before sending it out back to the client.

By default, this value is set to 1ms; in an environment with a lot of ICA-proxy sessions the network might be congested because of the high amount of small packets that need to be encapsulated.

Another important aspect of the SSL profile is determining the protocol to use. By default, a SSL-based vServer can communicate with SSL 3, TLS 1, TLS 1.1, and TLS 1.2.

As a recommendation, SSL 3 and TLS 1 should always be turned off because of security risks, and most clients and browsers today support the use of TLS 1.1 and 1.2.

Enable DH Param enables NetScaler to regenerate a new Diffie-Hellman private-public pair after a number of transactions. This feature needs to be enabled and defined to, for instance, a value of 1000; we also need to bind it with a DH key. This will make NetScaler regenerate a new key pair after 1,000 sessions to ensure that a malicious attacker cannot use a compromised DH key to get access to information.

Another aspect of SSL is the kind of ciphers to use. These ciphers decide what kind of protocol to use, what kind of encryption algorithm should be used, the key exchange algorithm, and what kind of message authentication code algorithm to use. These ciphers are not defined in SSL profiles, but are defined under SSL settings for each vServer.

The different ciphers can be found under **Traffic Management | SSL | Cipher Groups**. In this eDocs article, we can see all the different ciphers and what works with the different protocols: `http://docs.citrix.com/en-us/netscaler/11/traffic-management/ssl/supported-ciphers-list-release-11.html`.

In order to test our SSL capabilities we can use a website called `https://www.ssllabs.com/` that can verify the level of security on our external web services.

HTTP/2 and SPDY

Much tuning can be done in the lower layers of the OSI model, but there is also much that can be done in the higher levels, such as the application layer. HTTP 1.1 is the standard protocol used today on the Web, but is slowly being replaced with the new HTTP/2 standard.

Google started a couple of years ago with creating a protocol called SPDY that is a multiplexing, binary protocol. Much of the work that was started there was ported into HTTP/2, now being worked on by the IETF.

Today, most web servers already support HTTP/2:

- Nginx
- Apache
- IIS Windows Server 2016

It also has the benefit of using GZIP or deflate on the transmission headers, which allows for less overhead; since the protocol is pure binary transmission data, it is not directly readable and is much easier to send across the wire. This of course requires a browser that supports HTTP/2, but the latest versions of Google Chrome, Internet Explorer, Microsoft Edge, and Firefox support this already.

 HTTP/2 is not supported on VPX, only on the MPX/SDX; in cases where HTTP/2 is enabled, it will fall back to the SPDY protocol.

There is also a common requirement that, in order to use HTTP/2, we need to have a TLS-enabled service; even though this is not a requirement from the HTTP/2 standard, most vendors have implemented this requirement.

If a client connects to a vServer that has the HTTP/2 and SPDY profile enabled, communication will follow this sequence:

- HTTP/2
- SPDY
- HTTP 1.1

In order to enable HTTP/2 and/or SPDY, we need to create a HTTP profile. This can be done under **System | Profiles | HTTP Profiles**.

Here we can change the following to enable HTTP/2 and SPDY. Choose ENABLED under the **SPDY** parameter, this will enable SPDY v2 and v3 and allow the client to negotiate between the two, then add the checkmark on **HTTP/2** as shown in the following screenshot:

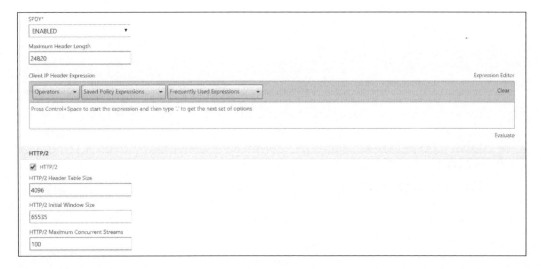

Monitoring network traffic

In some cases, we might need to monitor the network traffic between the endpoints and NetScaler for troubleshooting purposes, or just to ensure that the traffic flow is moving properly.

NetScaler has a number of built-in tools that we can use to gather information and for basic troubleshooting. For example, we have the regular tools such as `ping` and `traceroute` to verify network connectivity. We also have commands such as `show connectiontable`. This allows us to show connections in real-time and also can be used in conjunction with `grep` to make it easier to see if a particular client has a current connection with the NetScaler, for instance:

```
show connectiontable | grep -I "192.168.0.50" | grep -I "HTTP"
```

This will only display connections that are from `192.168.0.50` and are running over the HTTP protocol. We can also use the `show` command for other features as well such as ICA. We can use it to show if users are connected to an ICA session using the following commands:

```
show vpn icaconnection
```

```
show vpn stats
```

We also have some kernel commands such as `dmesg`, which will display all system message logs since the last reboot. For instance, if you are having IP-conflicts or a lot of `arp` based traffic, it will be displayed there.

Also NetScaler has a long list of different log files located under `/var/nslog` where it stores different content, such as the `newnslog` files.

We can use the `nsconmsg` command to report events in real time; we can also use the command to parse through statistical data. For instance, if we want to view old `newnslog` files, which NetScaler archives by default every two days, in order to view statistical data on our load-balanced vServers, we can use this command example:

```
nsconmsg -K /var/nslog/newnslog -d oldconmsg -s ConLb=2
```

This will run through the `newnslog`; the `-d` operator is to display performance data and the `-s ConLb=2` is for the level of load balancing events to display. The capital `K` means that it is read mode (typing a small `k` means write), which means that we might overwrite our log files.

In order to get real-time data and store it for further analysis, we have two options:

`nstrace.sh` and `nstcpdump.sh`

Both of them have different advantages and disadvantages depending on what information we need for further analysis.

Advantages of `nstrace.sh` include:

- Records network packet traces in the native NetScaler trace format, which provides specific NIC device information including the device number and whether the packet was transmitted or received
- Provides connection link information, allowing identification of links between client to virtual server and SNIP/MIP to server TCP connections
- Allows the creation of multiple files based on a set amount of time and number of files per cycle by using the `-nf` and `-time` options
- Allows the creation of separate trace files per NIC by using the `-nic` option

Disadvantages of `nstrace.sh` include:

- No ability to send packet capture data directly to `stdout` (standard output)

Advantages of `nstcpdump.sh` include:

- Ability to send packet capture data to `stdout` by omission of the `-w` option
- Allows use of standard `tcpdump` filters

Disadvantages of `nstcpdump.sh` include:

- Native NetScaler trace format is not supported
- `nstcpdump.sh` is more resource-intensive than `nstrace.sh` because this script runs both `nsapimgr`, to capture packets, and `tcpdump` to output data either to a file or to the screen

nstrace

We can start by looking more closely at `nstrace.sh`.

When analyzing traffic we should add a filter to ensure that we do not get overwhelmed by the information in the trace files. `nstrace` has a list of different parameters that we can use when running the command:

- `-time`: Duration of trace per file; default is `3600` seconds. Example: `-time 60`.
- `-tcpdump`: Defines if the trace file should be in `tcpdump` format; can either be enabled or disabled. Example: `-tcpdump ENABLED`.

- `-filesize`: Defines the size of the packet to be logged; maximum value can be `1514` and the default value is `164` headers only. Example: `-size 164`.

- `-perNIC`: Defines if the trace should create a trace file per NIC; this only works if the `-tcpdump` is set to `enabled`. Example: `-perNIC enabled`.

- `-name`: Defines a name for the trace file. Example: `-name test.pcap`.

- `-mode`: Defines the mode to use for capture; for instance `IPV6` - translated IPv6 packets; `NEW_RX` - received packets after NIC pipelining; `RX` - received packets before NIC pipelining; `TX` - transmitted packets; `TXB` - packets buffered for transmission. Example: `-mode -IPV6`.

- `-filter`: Here we can define different filters on what we want to get information about, which allows us to narrow down the trace file to contain only the bits of traffic we are interested in here; we have different qualifiers and operators we can use.

Qualifier	Value
SOURCEIP	IP address
SOURCEPORT	TCP port
DESTIP	IP address
DESTPORT	TCP port
SVCNAME	Service name
VSVRNAME	VServer name
VLAN	VLAN ID
STATE	CLOSE_WAIT, CLOSED, CLOSING, ESTABLISHED, FIN_WAIT_1, FIN_WAIT_2, LAST_ACK, LISTEN, SYN_RECEIVED, SYN_SENT, TIME_WAIT

We can also use the following operators on the different filters: `==`, `eq`, `!=`, `neq`, `>`, `gt`, `<`, `lt`, `>=`, `ge`, `<=`, `le`, and `BETWEEN`.

Also we can combine multiple sets of qualifiers can be used with Boolean `&&` or `||`.

Some examples on how we can set up `nstrace` to contain the traffic we want. For instance, let's say that we want to get all traffic coming from one particular IP address and one particular port, and we want to have all the data in the packets to do further analysis.

```
start nstrace -size 1514 -filter "SOURCEIP == 192.168.0.10 || SOURCEPORT
== 80" -link ENABLE
```

Or let's say that we want to get all the traffic going to a particular service on a NetScaler that seems to be getting a lot of traffic and we want to know what kind of traffic it is.

```
start nstrace –size 1514 –filter "SVCNAME == IIS"
```

The following table supplies a list of different examples illustrating the use of filters and operators to get the information we want:

Example command	Description
`start nstrace –filter "destport == 80"`	Get all traffic headed to port `80`
`start nstrace –filter "vsvrname == srv1"`	Get all traffic headed to virtual server `srv1`
`start nstrace –size 1514 –filter "SVCNAME == IIS" || "STATE == ESTABLISHED"`	Get all established TCP connections to service IIS with full packets
`start nstrace –filter "ip == 192.168.0.1 || ip == 192.168.0.2"`	Get all connections from IP addresses `192.168.0.1` and `192.168.0.2`

As I mentioned earlier, nstrace does not list live connection to the CLI; it only creates a trace file for further analysis. In order to get the trace files, we need to use an FTP client to get the trace files that are by default stored under /var/nstrace/DATE.

In order to analyze these trace files, we need a custom dissector in Wireshark, which we will cover a bit later in this chapter.

Now on the other hand we have nstcpdump.sh, the regular tcpdump that is built-in to the Unix OS.

nstcpdump

nstcpdump.sh allows for CLI output, meaning that we can see the traffic in real-time in the console. It is important to note however that nstcpdump uses the default parameters for tcpdump that are not the same as for nstrace.

For instance, `nstcpdump` has the following filter options:

- `host <IP_Address>`: To restrict recording of the packets to or from the specified host IP address.

- `net <Subnet_Address> mask <Netmask>`: To restrict recording of the packets from the specified subnet.

- `port <Port_Number>`: To restrict recording of the packets for the specified TCP or UDP port.

- `portrange <From_Port_Number>-<To_Port_Number>`: To restrict recording of the packets for the specified range of the TCP or UDP port numbers.

- `dst port <Port_Number>`: To restrict recording of the packets for the specified destination TCP or UDP port numbers.

- `src port <Port_Number>`: To restrict recording of the packets from the specified source TCP or UDP port numbers.

- `tcp`: To restrict recording of the packets only to the TCP packets. This option is a substitute for the `ip proto x` option.

- `udp`: To restrict recording of the packets only to the UDP packets.

- `arp`: To restrict recording of the packets only to the ARP packets.

- `icmp`: To restrict recording of the packets only to the ICMP packets.

 You can find the whole list of different operators, filters, and parameters here: `http://www.tcpdump.org/manpages/tcpdump.1.html`.

And now some example commands that we can use to get the current traffic. For instance, to get all traffic going to port `80`:

`nstcpdump.sh port 80`

Or to get all traffic coming from a particular host and going to a particular host:

`nstcpdump.sh src host 192.168.0.1 and dst host 192.168.0.2`

We can also use the parameter `-w` to write output to a `pcap` file:

`nstcpdump.sh -w /var/trace/trace1.cap`

We can also combine different parameters, for instance if we want to get traffic from a particular host that is on a particular interface and we want to store that information in a trace file:

```
nstcpdump.sh -w /var/trace/trace1.cap -I 1/1 src host 192.168.0.1
```

 Make sure that the folder we want to store the trace file in already exists before running the commands.

After we have created a trace file we need to analyze it using a packet manager, such as Wireshark or Microsoft Message Analyzer. If we are setting up Microsoft-based services, I recommend using Message Analyzer. For general analysis, I recommend using Wireshark, which will be covered in this book.

 In order to analyze nstrace files, which are Citrix-based trace files, we need to download the development version that contains support for reading these files. Wireshark can be downloaded from this website: www.wireshark.org.

Opening a nstrace file in Wireshark will give unique headers inside the packet, as shown in the following screenshot:

```
41 0.0264… 192.168.0.55   192.168.0.2    HTTP   302 HTTP/1.1 304 Not Modified [Packet size limited during capture]
42 0.0264… 192.168.0.55   192.168.0.2    TCP    318 [TCP Retransmission] 80→7790 [PSH, ACK] Seq=414 Ack=731 Win=8212 Len=213
43 0.0264… 192.168.0.55   192.168.0.2    HTTP   318 HTTP/1.1 304 Not Modified [Packet size limited during capture]
44 0.0269… 192.168.0.55   192.168.0.2    TCP    318 [TCP Retransmission] 80→51758 [PSH, ACK] Seq=414 Ack=702 Win=512 Len=213
45 0.0269… 192.168.0.55   192.168.0.2    TCP    302 [TCP Retransmission] 80→51758 [PSH, ACK] Seq=414 Ack=702 Win=512 Len=213
46 0.0269… 127.0.0.1      127.0.0.1      RSL    153 DEACTIVATE SACCH
47 0.0269… 127.0.0.1      127.0.0.1      TCP    169 [TCP Retransmission] 59747→5000 [PSH, ACK] Seq=673 Ack=961 Win=8212 Len=64
48 0.0269… 127.0.0.1      127.0.0.1      TCP    111 5000→59747 [ACK] Seq=961 Ack=737 Win=512 Len=0
49 0.0269… 127.0.0.1      127.0.0.1      RSL    169 DEACTIVATE SACCH
50 0.0389… 127.0.0.1      127.0.0.1      RSL    153 DEACTIVATE SACCH
51 0.0389… 127.0.0.1      127.0.0.1      TCP    169 [TCP Retransmission] 59747→5000 [PSH, ACK] Seq=737 Ack=1025 Win=8212 Len=64
52 0.0389… 127.0.0.1      127.0.0.1      TCP    111 5000→59747 [ACK] Seq=1025 Ack=801 Win=512 Len=0

> Frame 41: 302 bytes on wire (2416 bits), 199 bytes captured (1592 bits)
✓ NetScaler Packet Trace
   Operation: RX (0xae)
   Nic No: 2
 > Activity Flags: 0x00000000
 > Capture Flags: 0x00000000
   Errorcode: No Error (0x00)
   App: L2 (0x18)
   Core Id: 0
   Vlan: 0
   PcbDevNo: 0x00000000
   Linked PcbDevNo: 0x00000000
```

This allow us to see native NetScaler information such as the NIC, VLAN, and so on.

Analyzing network trace files using Wireshark

Wireshark contains a long list of different filters and options that we can use to analyze traffic from a trace file. Before we start going into analyzing the trace file, there are some settings we should configure before starting.

First, add a new column that shows, for instance, the destination port. All the different columns allow us to perform sorts and makes it easier to get the correct data.

This can be done by going into **Edit** | **Preferences** | **Appearance** | **Columns**. Click on the **+** sign and give it a name; click on the newly created column under **Type** and choose what kind of data that should be added, as shown in the following screenshot:

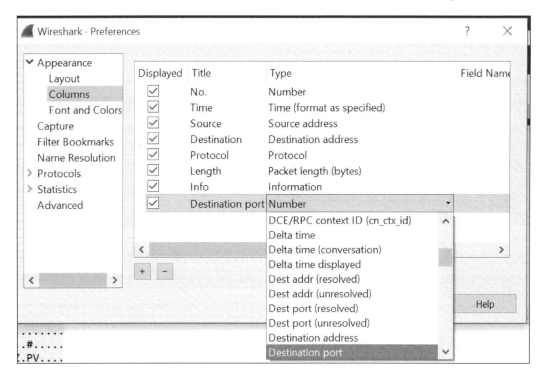

Next we need to enable name resolution. By default, a trace file does not resolve IP addresses into hostnames; therefore it might become cumbersome to analyze traffic without knowing where the traffic comes from.

We can enable this in Wireshark, and allow it to list all the IP addresses and query the DNS server that the Wireshark client is using to get all the hostnames. This can be enabled under **Preferences | Name Resolution**; enable **Resolve network (IP) addresses**, as shown in the following screenshot:

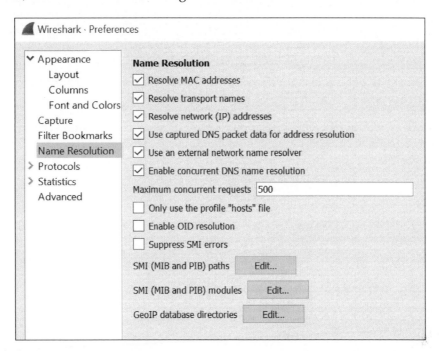

 We can also enable GeoIP-based filtering, which for instance allows us to filter traffic based upon country, organization, or region. This is useful with for instance DDoS attacks to find out where the traffic originated from.

Now after we have done the initial configuration, let's do some analysis on the trace file. For instance, if we have some issues with a client with the IP-address 192.168.0.2 that is unable to communicate with the vServer located on 192.168.0.80, we generate a trace file and open it in Wireshark.

The first thing we should do is filter the traffic in the trace file; this can be done using the following filter in the filter menu:

```
ip.src_host == 192.168.0.2 && ip.dst_host 192.168.0.80
```

This will display all packets coming from source `192.168.0.2` going towards IP `192.168.0.80`, and not traffic going back to the source IP.

> We cannot use IP filtering in Wireshark if we have DNS name resolution enabled. If we need to use hostnames, there is a good list of different filter options on the Wireshark wiki here: `https://wiki.wireshark.org/DisplayFilters`.

If for instance we were to use `ip.addr == 192.168.0.2`, we would see all traffic going from and to the IP address `192.168.0.2`.

When we have all the packets, we can right-click on a particular packet to get more options, as shown in the following screenshot:

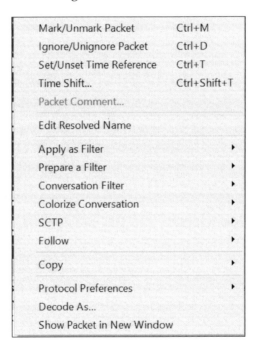

Mark/Unmark Packet	Ctrl+M
Ignore/Unignore Packet	Ctrl+D
Set/Unset Time Reference	Ctrl+T
Time Shift...	Ctrl+Shift+T
Packet Comment...	
Edit Resolved Name	
Apply as Filter	▶
Prepare a Filter	▶
Conversation Filter	▶
Colorize Conversation	▶
SCTP	▶
Follow	▶
Copy	▶
Protocol Preferences	▶
Decode As...	
Show Packet in New Window	

We can for instance choose to add more info to a particular filter and we can use the following option that allows us to actually see the particular conversation two hosts are having. For instance, if we have a HTTP-based TCP packet we can see in clear text what the traffic contains.

We can also see the TCP header information going back and forth between the endpoints; if we choose a particular TCP packet, we can see a lot of the different TCP parameters that we have enabled in the TCP profiles, as shown in the following screenshot:

```
> Frame 958: 101 bytes on wire (808 bits), 101 bytes captured (808 bits)
> NetScaler Packet Trace
> Ethernet II, Src: 192.168.0.2 (00:50:56:c0:00:01), Dst: 192.168.0.100 (00:0c:29:f9:25:5a)
> Internet Protocol Version 4, Src: 192.168.0.2 (192.168.0.2), Dst: 192.168.0.80 (192.168.0.80)
✓ Transmission Control Protocol, Src Port: 51765 (51765), Dst Port: http (80), Seq: 0, Len: 0
    Source Port: 51765 (51765)
    Destination Port: http (80)
    [Stream index: 16]
    [TCP Segment Len: 0]
    Sequence number: 0    (relative sequence number)
    Acknowledgment number: 0
    Header Length: 32 bytes
  > .... 0000 0000 0010 = Flags: 0x002 (SYN)
    Window size value: 8192
    [Calculated window size: 8192]
  > Checksum: 0xac34 [validation disabled]
    Urgent pointer: 0
  > Options: (12 bytes), Maximum segment size, No-Operation (NOP), Window scale, No-Operation (NOP), No-Operation (NOP), SACK permitted
```

Here we see that this is a `nstrace` file, and that we have adjusted the capture size so it does not capture all the data inside a packet. We can see what kind of MAC address the source and destination have. We can also see that this is an IPv4 packet that has a source address 192.168.0.2 and destination address of 192.168.0.80.

We can see the different TCP options such as destination port. We can also see that this is the first packet since it only contains SYN, which is the first step in the TCP handshake. We can see the window size value and that SACK is enabled.

If we go further down the packet list, we can also see the response and that the packet is sent as a response to a previous packet, as shown in the next screenshot:

```
✓ Transmission Control Protocol, Src Port: 51765 (51765), Dst Port: http (80), Seq: 1, Ack: 1, Len: 0
    Source Port: 51765 (51765)
    Destination Port: http (80)
    [Stream index: 16]
    [TCP Segment Len: 0]
    Sequence number: 1    (relative sequence number)
    Acknowledgment number: 1    (relative ack number)
    Header Length: 20 bytes
  > .... 0000 0001 0000 = Flags: 0x010 (ACK)
    Window size value: 64240
    [Calculated window size: 64240]
    [Window size scaling factor: -2 (no window scaling used)]
  > Checksum: 0xc766 [validation disabled]
    Urgent pointer: 0
  ✓ [SEQ/ACK analysis]
      [This is an ACK to the segment in frame: 964]
      [The RTT to ACK the segment was: 0.000824966 seconds]
      [iRTT: 0.000847641 seconds]
```

Wireshark can also list protocol-based information such as HTTP, which (for instance) allows us to see what kind of HTTP requests are being used. As seen in the following screenshot, we can see that a particular client is running a HTTP GET command, which is usually the case when a browser wants to get information from a web server:

```
∨ Hypertext Transfer Protocol
  ∨ GET / HTTP/1.1\r\n
    ∨ [Expert Info (Chat/Sequence): GET / HTTP/1.1\r\n]
      [GET / HTTP/1.1\r\n]
      [Severity level: Chat]
      [Group: Sequence]
    Request Method: GET
    Request URI: /
    Request Version: HTTP/1.1
  Host: 192.168.0.80\r\n
  Connection: keep-alive\r\n
  Accept: text/html,application/xhtml+xml,applicatio
  [Full request URI: http://192.168.0.80/]
  [HTTP request 1/1]
  [Packet size limited during capture: HTTP truncated]
```

So far we have seen that the HTTP request coming from 192.168.0.2 has gotten to the NetScaler and that the HTTP traffic is a legitimate HTTP GET command. Also we have seen that the client has gotten a response since the ACK indicated some traffic has been going to the backend service.

In Wireshark we have a built-in feature called **Expert Information**, which lists all warnings and error messages that appear in a trace file; this is useful to see (for instance) if we have duplicate IP addresses appearing in a trace or if TCP handshakes are not properly handled.

This option can be found under **Analyze | Expert Information** and is shown in the following screenshot:

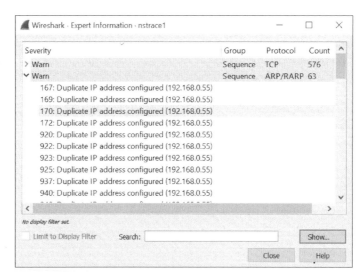

Duplicate IP addresses can also appear within the NetScaler console and will be stored in the logs. If we run the command we can get a list of all IP address conflicts:

```
nsconmsg -K /var/nslog/newnslog -d consmsg
```

We can see that the trace indicated that there are some issues as we have duplicate IP addresses configured. This menu will also list if there are TCP issues such as no response to SYN.

It is important to remember that NetScaler VPX is configured with two vNICs and that the IP addresses are floating across the different NICs; therefore it is quite common that you might get duplicate IP address messages from the NetScaler appliance itself unless properly configured.

The easiest way to troubleshoot a HTTP session, as in this example, is to follow the TCP stream. As mentioned earlier this can be done by right-clicking on a HTTP packet and selecting **Follow TCP Stream**; the result is shown in the following screenshot:

```
Wireshark · Follow TCP Stream (tcp.stream eq 26) · nstrace1

GET / HTTP/1.1
Host: 192.168.0.80
Connection: keep-alive
Cache-Control: max-age=0
Accept: text/html,applicHTTP/1.1 500 Internal Server Error
Content-Length: 71
Connection: close
Cache-Control: no-cache,no-store
P
```

The red text is communication from the client and the blue is the response from the backend server. The backend server is responding with an HTTP 500 error, which usually indicates that there is an issue with the backend web server.

Now in this example we used Wireshark to troubleshoot a HTTP session, which allows us to see traffic in readable text. In most cases we have encryption enabled using a SSL certificate that makes analyzing packets a bit more difficult.

With HTTP compression active, the HTTP data packets will also become scrambled since the data is compressed, thus making it harder to read data in real-text inside Wireshark. The same goes for HTTP/2, as it is in essence a binary protocol.

With Wireshark, we can actually decrypt HTTPS packets in the trace files as long as we have the private key from the digital certificate that was used on the vServer.

You will only need to download the private key from NetScaler if you have created a certificate from scratch; it can be easily downloaded from NetScaler by navigating to **Traffic Management | SSL | Manage Certificates | Keys**. If you have a PFX file, you need to use OpenSSL to export the private key from it. OpenSSL can also be found under the **SSL** pane. From there, run the following command:

```
openssl.exe pkcs12 -in publicAndprivate.pfx -nocerts -out    privateKey.
pem
```

This can also be started from the CLI. So after we get hold of the private key, we need to add it to Wireshark. In Wireshark, go to **Edit | Preferences | Protocols | SSL**. There, under the RSA keys list, choose **Edit**. Then from there choose **New**. Now we have to enter the IP address of the vServer, which appears in the trace files we want to decrypt. Also, we need to enter the port nr, which is 443, and the protocol, which is http. Then point it to the private key that has been downloaded from NetScaler.

Then choose **Apply**; Wireshark will then update the trace logs with the decrypted data. And we can now once again use filters to locate the particular conversation between the client and the vServer.

We can also use Wireshark to determine the amount of traffic going through a particular network card or the amount of bandwidth being used for a particular client. After we have added a filter in Wireshark we can go into **Statistics | Capture file properties**.

Here we can see information regarding the trace file itself and the amount of data being processed; we can also see specific information about the packets that are filtered, which is a good way to find out how much traffic has been consumed to handle one client.

Analyzing network traffic using Citrix NetScaler® Insight

Now, in most cases, NetScaler is used as a central component to deliver high availability services to users, both internally and externally. This means that NetScaler, in most cases, handles a large amount of traffic, which might make it difficult to analyze directly using a trace file.

What happens if a user complains about the slow performance of an application, or that something is running sluggishly? Or if we want to get an overview of the number of users accessing our services? This is where AppFlow comes in. A quick introduction to deployment is supplied in *Chapter 3, Integration with Citrix® Components*.

AppFlow is a feature in NetScaler that is used to collect web performance data and also database information. It can also be used to gather performance from ICA sessions. It is built upon the IPFIX format, which is an open standard defined in RFC 5101.

As an example, see the following screenshot. When a client opens a connection to the VIP of NetScaler, it will perform a new connection to the backend server and then the traffic is returned from the backend server back to NetScaler and thence to the client.

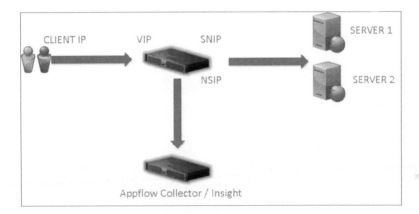

The AppFlow feature will send data to a collector with information about the client that connected; this is shown in the previous screenshot. The information includes the port and service it accessed and what backend server it got connected to. So we have a complete overview of all the conversations that a client has with a service.

By default, NetScaler uses its NSIP to deliver data to an AppFlow collector. It is important to note that we can use net profiles to tell AppFlow to use another IP address—for instance, a SNIP.

Viewing the AppFlow data requires that we have a collector that is capable of analyzing the data. Some vendors have tools capable of processing AppFlow data. These include:

- Solarwinds: http://www.solarwinds.com/products/freetools/AppFlow-jflow-sflow-analyzer.aspx
- Splunk app for AppFlow https://splunkbase.splunk.com/app/370/

And Citrix has its own product called NetScaler Insight, which is a separate download from Citrix.

NetScaler Insight is a virtual appliance that is supported on the same hypervisor platforms as NetScaler VPX. When setting up the appliance from version 11, there are some major changes from the previous versions. It is now much easier to set up a scaled-out environment, using different Insight components.

Insight consist of three different components:

- **Agents**: These are used to communicate with the different NetScaler and CloudBridge appliances and will then forward AppFlow logs to the connectors. These agents are only used for HTTP-based traffic flows.
- **Connectors**: Connectors receive AppFlow data from the different agents that will then be spread evenly between the different backend database servers.
- **Database**: The database node receives and stores data coming from the different connectors.

We can select the role we want to configure when deploying the virtual appliance. We also have a fourth role called Insight Center that is used to orchestrate all three roles. When setting up Insight for the first time, we always need to have the Insight Center server first, since the other roles reference Insight Center for deployment. We need to have all four components in place before we can properly configure Insight.

```
NetScaler Insight Deployment Type. This menu allow you to set an
ent type.
Selecting the listed number allows deployment type selected.
-------------------------------------------------------------------
    1. NetScaler Insight Server.
    2. Connector Node.
    3. Database Node.
    4. NetScaler Insight Agent.
    5. Cancel and quit.

Select a choice from 1 to 5 [5]: 1
```

It is important to note that the amount of data the Insight appliance stores depends on what kind of license the NetScaler appliances are running. If we have the NetScaler Standard license and we wish to use it with Insight, we can only use the Web Insight functionality. If we have NetScaler Enterprise, we can use Web Insight but the HDX Insight data will only show traffic for the last month. If we have NetScaler Platinum, we can use Web Insight and HDX Insight and will be able to show traffic for the last year.

After we have configured what kind of deployment we need, we can continue with the administration from the Web GUI; the default username and password is `nsroot`. At first login we can run through the wizard to add a NetScaler appliance using its NSIP, from which we can configure AppFlow data.

After successfully connecting to a NetScaler, the wizard will list all load-balancing, content-switching, cache redirections, and VPN vServers that are on the appliance. We can right-click on a vServer and choose to enable AppFlow. For VPN-based servers we only need to set an expression to `true`, which means that all VPN sessions will be forwarded using AppFlow, as shown in the following screenshot:

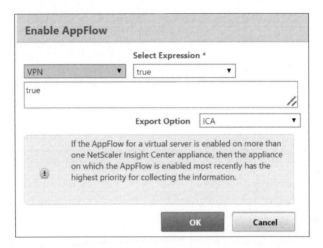

For load-balancing-based vServers, we have more granular control on the kind of data that should be forwarded to the AppFlow collector. We can use for instance the name of the vServer or hostname and so on, as shown in the following screenshot:

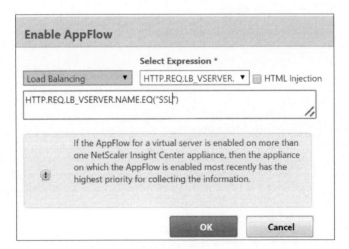

We can also use the general expression `true`.

Enable **HTML Injection** to get L7 metrics line Load Time, Render Time Response Time, Client Network Latency, Server Network Latency and Server Processing Time.

After enabling AppFlow collection for both vServers, we can see on the NetScaler appliance that an AppFlow collector has been added under **System | AppFlow | Collectors**. And that we have some policies in place; these are to ensure that AppFlow data will be generated for both vServers.

If you enable AppFlow on a HA-pair, it might disconnect ICA sessions when doing failover; this is documented in the following CTX article, and at the time of writing has not been fixed: `http://support.citrix.com/article/CTX201524`.

In the latest release of NetScaler Insight we can now integrate it with the Google geo coding API in order to get geo information about clients who are connecting to our vServers. This requires the GeoLite database, which can be downloaded from: `http://geolite.maxmind.com/download/geoip/database/GeoLiteCity.dat.gz`.

After we have set up the four virtual appliances and added a NetScaler appliance, we need to deploy the Insight configuration. Go into **Configuration | NetScaler Insight Center | Insight Deployment Management |** click on the **X** button in the top menu and then click **Deploy**. This will set up the deployment according to the different roles we have configured.

After the deployment is done and the appliance is restarted, Insight's setup should look like the following screenshot:

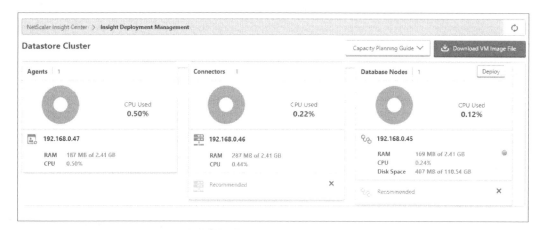

Now we need to adjust part of the configuration. By default, logging for Web Insight is disabled because this might generate a huge amount of data. In order to enable it, we need to go into the **Insight appliance** | **Configuration** | **System**, change data log record settings, and enable Web Insight logs from there.

We should also enable URL data collection, which allows Insight to gather all the different URLs used in the session info for the database; this can be enabled under the same path but under change URL data collection settings.

There are also some other settings that define what kind of data we see in the dashboard, which can be enabled under **Configuration** | **System**, change Web Insight reports settings.

After we have configured the basic settings and have AppFlow enabled on the appliance, when we generate a session against the AppFlow-enabled service, data should start appearing on the dashboard in Insight Center, as shown in the following screenshot:

We can now see the different AppFlow data that is being generated from NetScaler; this allows us to see performance data and other information such as:

- HTTP response status
- Client latency settings
- Server latency settings
- Response time
- Server processing time

- What kind of URL and servers have been accessed
- IP address of the client and what type of browser has been used
- Content type

The same goes with HDX Insight part of the dialog, where we get information such as:

- **WAN latency**: This is the average latency caused by the client-side network
- **DC latency**: This is the average latency caused by the server network
- **ICA RTT**: This is the average screen lag that the user experiences while interacting with an application or desktop hosted on XenApp or XenDesktop
- **Bandwidth**: This is the rate at which data is transferred over the ICA session

All this information allows us to get information on a particular client, and makes it a lot easier for us to troubleshoot any client-related issues—for instance, if a client is having issues connecting but we can see from within Insight that the client has a high amount of latency. If we also combine this with GeoInsight, this allows us to see, for instance, the amount of time it takes to go from the US to Europe.

In most cases we want to have HDX Insight available inside Citrix Director, since this is the common troubleshooting tool for XenApp/XenDesktop administrators. In order to configure this integration, we need to run this command on the Director server `C:\inetpub\wwwroot\Director\tools\DirectorConfig.exe` with the parameter `/confignetscaler`.

Troubleshooting NetScaler® Insight

Getting Insight to work properly requires that everything is configured properly, and there might be something that gets in the way of this. Here is a list of common issues that might block AppFlow from working:

- **NTP time sync**: Make sure that NTP sync is set up and configured properly. If we need to configure time manually on the Insight appliance, login using CLI and use the command `date`. Make also sure that the time zones are correct.
- **UDP port 4739**: AppFlow uses UDP to deliver data to the collector; make sure that any firewall or ACL has UDP port 4739 open to ensure that data is being sent.
- **AppFlow policy hit**: Double-check the AppFlow policies on the NetScaler appliance and see if they are generating any hits. This ensures that the configured expression is configured properly.

- **AppFlow enabled on the vServer and services**: Make sure that AppFlow is enabled on services and virtual servers. This can be verified most easily using the CLI command `show vServer | grep "Appflow"` and for services `show service | grep "Appflow"`.

- **If a particular user is not being displayed in the HDX Insight part**: Ensure that the user is using the latest version of Citrix Receiver.

- **WAN and DC latency show up as zero**: This is intended; latency below 1 MS will be displayed as zero.

- **Web insight logs not showing**: Make sure that we enable Web Insight logging on the Insight configuration, since it is disabled by default.

> Citrix Insight Services now supports NetScaler Insight, which allows for automatic troubleshooting of the most common issues. More information can be found on `http://cis.citrix.com`, and we will be covering Insight Services in the next chapter.

Summary

In this chapter, we have gone through different tuning and optimization features such as TCP profiles, SSL profiles, jumbo frames, and so on. Then we went on to discuss how to monitor network traffic using built-in tools such as `nstrace` and `nstcpdmp`, and lastly we explored how we can use NetScaler Insight to monitor end-to-end performance.

In the next chapter we will examine in greater depth the different security features inside NetScaler and how we can use them to protect our various services.

6
Security Features and Troubleshooting

NetScaler often sits in front of large web services processing large amount of data; some of these services may contain credit card transactions or serve sensitive data. It is therefore crucial that NetScaler is properly configured to protect the data. Also, with this large amount of data going through the application we might be required to troubleshoot network traffic or a session in general.

The following are some of the subjects that we will go through in this chapter:

- Management best practices
- Protecting against DDoS attacks
- SSL and TLS best practices
- Admin partitions
- Auditing and AAA
- Citrix Insight Services

Management best practices for security

Before configuring NetScaler for any type of service, we should always ensure that NetScaler is locked down in way that management access can be brute-forced, MitM attacks for logging and so on. So as a best-practice we should:

- Disable interfaces that are not used.
- Do not start any features that we do not use.
- Define a SNMP manager we can send alerts to. Prefer using SNMPv3, which allows for encrypted authentication and traffic.

- Disable heartbeat monitoring on disabled interfaces in HA setup.

- Change the nsroot password.

- Set up external authentication access to NetScaler, which allows for AD group authentication to NetScaler and makes it easier to audit and control changes; it also restricts access. In order to set up this feature we can follow this Citrix article http://support.citrix.com/article/CTX123782. It is important to make sure that this feature is bound to a global level and that the nsroot account is marked as non-external authentication access. If not, an admin can create an nsroot account in Active Directory and then have full admin access on NetScaler.

- Use SSL/TLS authentication to LDAP whenever possible as well.

- Disable management access on regular HTTP and allow only secure access. This can be done under **System | IPs** | nsip; mark the checkbox to allow **Secure Access Only**.

- Set up Secure NTP to allow for encrypted NTP traffic; also we can configure the NTP daemon to prevent traffic amplification attack using the instructions here: http://support.citrix.com/article/CTX200286.

- Switch to public key authentication when using SSH with NetScaler http://support.citrix.com/article/CTX109011.

- Set up an external syslog server to gather errors and information logs from a NetScaler appliance; or use Command Center from Citrix, for instance.

- Enable ARP spoof validation to ensure that no L4 device can spoof a MAC address. This can be enabled under **System | Network** | configure global arp parameters.

- Create a custom SSH banner for those logging in using SSH: http://support.citrix.com/article/CTX124517.

- Disable ICMP for virtual IP-addresses, unless required. ICMP scanning is a commonly used tool to scan for live hosts; disabling ICMP on all VIP might reduce the number of attacks.

- Disable SSH access to NetScaler via SNIP; this is a default option that enables SSH for all SNIP addresses. This can be disabled on each SNIP address.

- Create a full backup each time we do a change to the configuration. Remember that, if we make a change and manage to lock ourselves out we can reboot NetScaler and get back to the state before we changed the config. If we did not manage the save the configuration, since changes are first stored in the running configuration and that we have to save it to stored configuration. It is also important to have a config backup stored on network-based storage in case of emergency; this can be done under **System | Backup and Restore**. These backups can either be downloaded using web management or by using SFTP to the host and copying the folders under /var/ns_sys_backup.

- Configure secure RPC communication. By default NetScaler appliances in a HA-setup or GSLB setup communicate without encryption using RPCI. In order to switch to secure communication we can configure this under System | Network | rpc, and secure. Note that we have to configure this on the other appliances as well.

- Try to keep NetScaler up to date. Citrix releases new builds and many of these builds might contain security fixes for known vulnerabilities; they might also contain performance fixes/features and so on. However, do not rush to implement the latest version as some builds might cause other issues. It is important to read the release notes to see if there are other issues with the newest builds before upgrading.

- If we place NetScaler in a virtual environment, disable ARP protection for it, since a NetScaler might have multiple IP-addresses from the same MAC address originating from a single port, which might trigger the virtualization protection features.

Security features in NetScaler®

Since NetScaler often sits in front of many different services, this might make it a popular target for hackers. This might for instance affect PCI-DSS services, such as VISA or PayPal. Or just plain web services, perhaps an intranet portal or some other sort of sensitive data.

So the goal is to configure NetScaler to deflect common forms of attack and activate counter-measures when someone is trying a particular form of attack.

A popular question that is often asked is: should NetScaler be in front of the firewall or should the firewall be the first line of defense?

NetScaler has many prebuilt defense mechanisms against, for instance, **Denial of Service (DoS)** attacks on the TCP layer. The default TCP profile `nstcp_default_profile` has a setting called **TCP SYN Cookie** that in essence stops DDoS attacks using **TCP SYN Flood**.

Under **TCP Profiles** we also have the option to enable **SYN Spoof Protection**, this feature is not enabled by default but it can help NetScaler to stop attacks coming from spoofed SYN packets.

We have some similar capabilities under **HTTP Profiles**. In the default `nshttp_default_profile` we can for instance enable **Drop invalid HTTP requests**, which helps against HTTP attacks if the requests are not following the proper standard.

HTTP DoS protection

In some cases, it might not be that easy to detect an attack. For instance, in a HTTP DDoS attack, a web server might be attacked with legitimate traffic; therefore they are regular HTTP requests. This is where we can use HTTP DoS protection. HTTP DoS protection allow NetScaler to respond with a JavaScript challenge to all incoming HTTP requests. Since a HTTP DDoS attack is typically done using a cluster of many nodes running a scripted attack, these nodes do not support any form of JavaScript request; therefore, when they cannot respond to the JavaScript challenge, NetScaler closes the connection. Regular users surfing with a regular browser support JavaScript and are therefore granted access. This happens in the background and the user never sees that it happens. Enabling HTTP DoS puts a lot of strain on NetScaler, especially if there is a lot of traffic and the client detect rate is at 100 percent.

In order to enable HTTP DoS, go into **Security | Protection Features | HTTP DoS** and click **Add**.

Then give the policy a name and enter a queue depth that is a representation of the number of outstanding requests to the system, before the HTTP DoS feature is enabled. Then we should enter a client detect rate; this is a percent value between 0 and 100 to define what percentage of requests after the HTTP DoS feature is triggered should get the JavaScript challenge.

> By default, the value is set to 1 percent in the global HTTP DoS parameters.

After we have created a HTTP DoS policy we have to bind it to our services. Go into **Traffic Management | Services**, then choose the services we want this enabled for, then go into **Policies** and click the **+** sign and choose **HTTP DoS** and find the newly created policy.

It is also important that we have defined thresholds on NetScaler services; otherwise, NetScaler cannot know how many requests or clients the backend services can handle and the HTTP DoS feature will never trigger.

Setting these values can be done under **Services** | **Thresholds**.

Access-lists

NetScaler also has support for the traditional access-list where we can define four types of lists. All of them have the option to define protocol, but simple ACLs only support TCP/UDP while extended ACLs have a long list of different protocols such as EGP, ICMP, GRE, and so on:

- Simple ACL, which defines only DENY rules for source IP addresses.
- Simple ACL6, which defines only DENY rules for source IPv6 addresses.
- Extended ACL, which allow us to define DENY/ALLOW/BRIDGE rules for source ip, source-range and destination ip, and destination ip-range. It also allows us to configure the source MAC and destination MAC.
- Extended ACL6, which allows us to define DENY/ALLOW/BRIDGE rules for source IPv6, source-range and destination IPv6, and destination IPv6-range. It also allows us to configure the source MAC and destination MAC.

Simple ACLs are only stored in memory and cannot be seen in the running configuration; so, when we define a simple ACL, it has a TTL of eight seconds and therefore can expire and be deleted. Simple ACLs are very memory-effective and should therefore only be used to block out single IP addresses for a period of time.

Extended ACLs do not have an expiration timer and give more granular control over where we want to ALLOW/DENY traffic.

An extended ACL example in the CLI might look like this:

```
add ns acl ext_block_bad_ip ALLOW -srcIP = 100.0.0.0-101.0.0.255
-protocol TCP -priority 10
```

By default, an ACL is not active; this can be seen by running a show ACL and viewing the effective status on it. In order to apply an ACL, we need to append the -kernelstate APPLIED parameter to the end of the command. It is however important to remember that the packet processing that takes place on NetScaler will run a packet through on any eventual simple ACLs first before they are then evaluated against the extended ACLs.

In order to see the status of the ACL we can use the CLI command:
`show acl`

SSL settings

In order to ensure a high level of security we need to properly configure the SSL settings on NetScaler. Over the last couple of years there have been many known vulnerabilities in the SSL protocol that could allow for man-in-the-middle attacks. These included for instance Heartbleed, Beast, and so on.

But with the growing list of known vulnerabilities, it might be difficult to get an overview in order to ensure that our services are properly configured for the highest level of security.

Ssllabs.com (`https://www.ssllabs.com/`) offers a free service that allows us to test our external web services for SSL configuration. It tests all of the known vulnerabilities in the SSL/TLS protocol, and also tests different ciphers and the certificate.

So a good best practice is to configure our SSL settings to get an A+ score on the ssllabs test. In order to get A+ we need to do some changes to the default SSL settings:

- Disable SSL 3
- Enable TLS 1.2
- RC4 ciphers must be disabled
- Prefer EC DH ciphers
- Server Certificate with SHA2/SHA256 support (needs to be purchased from a vendor supporting these types of certificate)
- Enable HTTP Strict Transport Security

Let us start by disabling SSL 3 and enabling TLS 1.2. Up until v11, the VPX could not support TLS 1.1 or 1.2 but now it can. There are two ways to enable/disable the different protocols: either using SSL profiles or defining SSL parameters on vServer.

Using SSL profiles allows us to more easily create a profile for frontend/backend services, which was covered in the previous chapter, while SSL parameters are only available on the individual vServer.

TLS 1.1 and TLS 1.2 are not available on a backend SSL profile on a VPX, and defining a SSL profile on a vServer will override the SSL parameters.

In the **SSL Profile** we should:

- Disable SSL 3
- Enable TLS 1.1 & 1.2
- Set **Deny SSL Renegotiation** to NONSECURE
- Define the frontend

 It is important that TLS 1 is still enabled if the SSL profile is going to be bound to a NetScaler Gateway vServer since the receiver only supports TLS 1, not 1.1 and 1.2.

Next we need to create a SSL cipher list with different options, which is easiest done using CLI. This first example is aimed at MPX:

```
add ssl cipher cipher-list-mpx
bind ssl cipher cipher-list-mpx -cipherName TLS1.2-ECDHE-RSA-AES256-GCM-SHA384
bind ssl cipher cipher-list-mpx -cipherName TLS1.2-ECDHE-RSA-AES128-GCM-SHA256
bind ssl cipher cipher-list-mpx -cipherName TLS1.2-ECDHE-RSA-AES-256-SHA384
bind ssl cipher cipher-list-mpx -cipherName TLS1.2-ECDHE-RSA-AES-128-SHA256
bind ssl cipher cipher-list-mpx -cipherName TLS1-ECDHE-RSA-AES256-SHA
bind ssl cipher cipher-list-mpx -cipherName TLS1-ECDHE-RSA-AES128-SHA
bind ssl cipher cipher-list-mpx -cipherName TLS1.2-DHE-RSA-AES256-GCM-SHA384
bind ssl cipher cipher-list-mpx -cipherName TLS1.2-DHE-RSA-AES128-GCM-SHA256
bind ssl cipher cipher-list-mpx -cipherName TLS1-DHE-RSA-AES-256-CBC-SHA
bind ssl cipher cipher-list-mpx -cipherName TLS1-DHE-RSA-AES-128-CBC-SHA
bind ssl cipher cipher-list-mpx -cipherName TLS1-AES-256-CBC-SHA
bind ssl cipher cipher-list-mpx -cipherName TLS1-AES-128-CBC-SHA
bind ssl cipher cipher-list-mpx -cipherName SSL3-DES-CBC3-SHA
```

The second example is aimed at VPX instances, version 11:

```
add ssl cipher vpx11
bind ssl cipher vpx11 -cipherName TLS1-ECDHE-RSA-AES256-SHA
bind ssl cipher vpx11 -cipherName TLS1-ECDHE-RSA-AES128-SHA
bind ssl cipher vpx11 -cipherName TLS1-DHE-RSA-AES-256-CBC-SHA
bind ssl cipher vpx11 -cipherName TLS1-DHE-RSA-AES-128-CBC-SHA
bind ssl cipher vpx11 -cipherName TLS1-AES-256-CBC-SHA
bind ssl cipher vpx11 -cipherName TLS1-AES-128-CBC-SHA
bind ssl cipher vpx11 -cipherName SSL3-DES-CBC3-SHA
```

Now, when we need to configure this on a SSL server, we need to add the SSL profile and the unique cipher list that we created, as shown in the next screenshot:

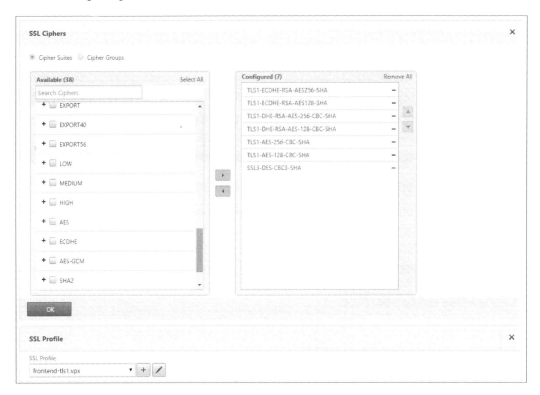

The last piece of the puzzle is to implement **Enable HTTP Strict Transport Security**. HTST is a novel protocol complement to HTTPS that allows a website owner to make https the only method that the browser may use for accessing the site. Also, it enforces certificate integrity.

The way to enable this is by using a rewrite policy. Create a new rewrite action with the following values:

- **Name**: Namefortheaction
- **Type**: INSERT_HTTP_HEADER
- **Header Name**: Strict-Transport-Security
- **String Expression**: "\"max-age=157680000\""

Next we create a rewrite policy that binds the action to a policy. The important part here is that we use the expression TRUE, which indicates that all traffic should have this rewrite policy enabled.

After we have created the policy we need to bind it to the vServer we want to have it enabled for.

Admin partitions

Admin partitions is one of the new features in NetScaler; it allows an appliance to be partitioned into logical entities called admin partitions, where each partition can be configured and used as a separate NetScaler appliance; we can then allow superusers to access and configure their own partition.

This allows for separated partitions to, for instance, Microsoft Exchange, SQL, SharePoint and web application owners, and so on.

Each partition has its own file structure where it stores configuration files for that partition, located under /nsconfig/partitions/<partitionName>. SSL certificates are stored under /var/partitions/<partitionName>/netscaler/ssl.

Also each partition has its own set of resources that is defined during setup.

> There are still some limits on what features that can be configured in admin partitions; this includes the application firewall, NetScaler gateway, AAA-TM, Load balancing for FTP, SIP, RADIUS, RDP, VXLAN, Cluster, DNS, GSLB, and so on. You can view the non-supported features here: https://docs.citrix.com/en-us/netscaler/11/system/admin-partition/admin-partition-config-types.html.

In order to segregate network traffic, we can bind a partition either to a particular VLAN or a Bridge Group.

To create a new partition, go to **System | Partition Administrator | Partitions | Add**, from there give the partition a name and define the amount of resources that this partition should have access to.

 Integrated Caching is a supported feature in NS11 so, if we want to use caching on a partition, it is important that we define enough memory for the partition.

Then afterwards we should bind it to a VLAN, which is again either bound to an IP or interface. If we have an MPX with multiple interfaces it is common to bind a particular VLAN to an interface that is then bound to a partition. It is important to note that a VLAN can only be bound to one partition at a time.

Then we need to add a user with access to this partition. As of now in version 11 we cannot use external user access to a partition; this needs to be a local user on NetScaler.

When creating the new user, we can either define the user rights directly using system command policy or we can bind the user to an existing NetScaler group if we have one. Shown in the following screenshot are the different built-in user roles that define what kind of access/commands a user has:

By clicking on a role and choosing **Edit**, we can see which command sets a role has access to. We can also define our own user role by clicking **Add** and then going into Command Spec Editor. Here we can define custom access roles based upon features, which can then be bound to a partition. It is important to note here that, if we choose the non-partition user roles, they will have access to switching between partitions. If we want to define a user as having admin privileges only on the partition, we can use the partition-admin role.

Now, after we have defined a user role and bound it to a user, we can click **Done**. In order to switch partitions, we have a quick-switch option in the top menu, as shown in the next screenshot. This option is available for superusers/sysadmins:

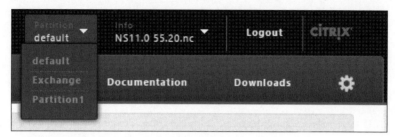

Partition-administrators can access their partition using the same web management URL or using CLI. When they connect to their partition, they will have the name of the partition they are on set as the title.

 Support for CLI mode is not complete yet; therefore a partition user who tries accessing NetScaler using CLI might get an error message saying: **Operation not permitted**.

Analyzing issues using Citrix® Insight Services

Citrix Insight Service is a free cloud service from Citrix that allow us to upload detailed logging information and configuration from NetScaler and scan it against a set of rules to see if there are any issues or best-practices that we have not configured. It is also often used in conjunction with Citrix support cases; Citrix will often tell you to upload data to Insight Services before they can continue troubleshooting.

In order to generate log files for Citrix Insight Services, we need to go into **System | Diagnostics**, and then from there click on **Generate support file**. Or we can use the command:

```
show techsupport
```

This will generate a `tar.gz` under the folder `/var/tmp/support/collector_ ip_data.tar.gz`, which can be downloaded to a local machine using for instance WinSCP or any other FTP-based client.

> You can also enable a feature called Call Home, which will allow NetScaler to automatically upload a tech support `tar.gz` to Insight Services in the case of a critical error or failure.
>
> This can be done using the CLI command:
>
> `set callhome -emailaddress email@domain.com`

This requires that NetScaler has a way to communicate externally and with a default gateway set.

After we have download the `tar.gz` file we need to upload it to Insight Services. Go to `https://taas.citrix.com/AutoSupport/`. From here we need to login with our Citrix account, then we need to choose **Upload data**. When we choose **Upload data** we have the option to enter a case number, if we have a troubleshooting support case with Citrix, but in our case just click on **Upload data**.

Then it will take a couple of minutes to do the analysis; for larger scenarios it might take more time. TaaS will notify you with an e-mail to your contact address (listed with the Citrix account) after it has completed the analysis.

Now when the analysis is done it can go through the running configuration and give us some feedback regarding best-practices on our instance, as shown in the following screenshot:

NetScaler Overview	Health Check Summary	
Health Check Summary	**Diagnostic Report (7 live alerts)**	
Appliance Overview		
NetScaler Environment	We are constantly feeding Insight Services new problem and best practices definitions. If we haven't solved your issue or Click here to open a case with Support (support contract required), or search our Knowledge Base.	
Environment Diffing		
	Issue Name: Integrated Caching memory limit	
	Description: Integrated Caching memory limit is either set to 0 or is more than 50% of system memory.	
	Issue Name: Crash file found on NetScaler	
	Description: Crash file has been detected on the NetScaler appliance. The core files are located in /var/core directory.	
	Issue Name: A VPN Virtual Server is in DOWN state due to missing certificate key pair bound to it.	
	Description: Upgrade / downgrade of appliance firmware could cause certkey pair bindings to disappear and VPN vserver to go DOWN.	
	Issue Name: 1519-Drop invalid HTTP requests NetScaler 10x	
	Description: NetScaler defaults to allowing all HTTP requests. Best practice is to drop invalid HTTP requests or responses	

We can also do a drill-down on each of the different alerts to get more detailed information about a state and even command line examples on how we can fix the issues. We can also get a detailed overview of performance on NetScaler, CPU, packets, memory, and so on. Citrix is also doing a lot of work on this feature; Insight Services now also supports NetScaler Insight.

Setting up AAA – authentication and authorization

The AAA feature allows us to set up NetScaler as an authentication point in front of different Web-services. This might be Microsoft Exchange, Microsoft SharePoint, or any other load-balanced web service where we want to define NetScaler to do the initial authentication using an AAA vServer and then do an SSO backend to the resource, as shown in the next screenshot:

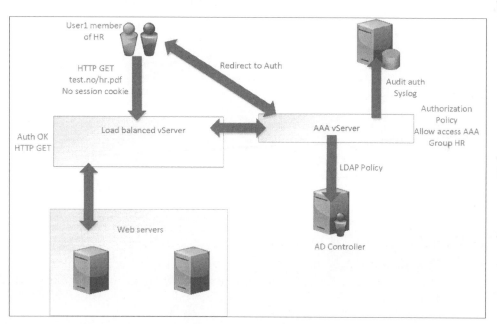

We can also define within NetScaler what the user is allowed to access on the backed resource using the authorization module, where we can restrict for instance access to PDF files based upon an expression.

Now we can create an AAA vServer that the users are redirected to. Go into the **AAA – Application Traffic** pane, click on **Virtual Servers**, and click **Add**.

Here under the settings we need to enter a name, IP-address, and port number. By default, it is set to SSL and 443. We also have an optional parameter: authentication domain. Here we need to enter the FQDN of the AAA vServer if we want to use form-based authentication.

Form-based authentication is an authentication mechanism that is wrapped around combining HTTP and HTML code, where a user enters his/her user information in web forms and clicks **Submit**.

If we click the **More** button, we also have some additional parameters that we need to consider:

- Failed login timeouts
- Max login attempts

These define the amount of times a user can try to authenticate against a vServer, and eventually how long the user will be locked out if they have tried too many times. By default, these values are not set but should be configured in order to reduce the amount of attacks, for instance dictionary attacks or brute force attacks.

After we are done entering the values we can click **Continue**. Now we are prompted to enter a server certificate and a CA certificate. These need to be added before the virtual server can become active.

After we have added both we can start defining authentication policies. These policies define how NetScaler should authenticate users who try to access it—for instance, whether it should be based upon LDAP, RADIUS, SAML, and so on. This is defined by an expression that NetScaler needs to evaluate when receiving the connection.

Authentication policy

Let us start by creating a basic authentication policy using LDAP that will allow our users to login using their Active Directory credentials when they are redirected to the AAA vServer. First click on the **+** sign and choose **LDAP** and **Primary type**.

In the expression pane, write ns_true. This means that all traffic that enters this vServer will get this policy. Then click on the **+** sign on the server and enter the information on the Active Directory server.

After we have finished adding an LDAP server and are through with the LDAP policy, we can go into **Authentication | Dashboard** to see the status of our LDAP servers.

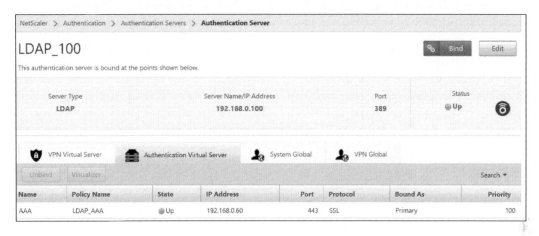

From here we can see that the server is responding to LDAP and that it is bound to a particular AAA vServer.

Now that we have created an AAA vServer and added a basic LDAP authentication policy, we need to bind it to a service that we want to have authentication on.

An AAA vServer can either be bound to a Content Switching vServer or a load-balanced vServer; in my example we have a load-balanced vServer.

Go into the **vServer | Edit | Choose Authentication** pane on the right side.

Now we have two options; either choose **Form based authentication** or **401 based authentication**. Form-based authentication will present a Citrix based login page that allows users to enter a username and password into HTML forms that will then be authenticated against the LDAP policy we have; this type of authentication will create a session ID that will be stored on the client browser. 401-based authentication uses HTTP to present a dialog box on the browser where we enter our username and password.

 401 based authentication is the same as basic authentication in IIS.

For now, we are going to use form-based authentication. Since this presents a web page, we need to enter the FQDN of the AAA vServer since NetScaler will redirect users to that particular vServer.

Then choose an authentication virtual server type, set that to `Authentication Virtual Server`, and then choose the `AAA` vServer in the drop-down menu below. We also have an alternative option called **Authentication profile** but this is covered a bit later in this chapter.

Now the configuration should look like this on the load-balanced vServer:

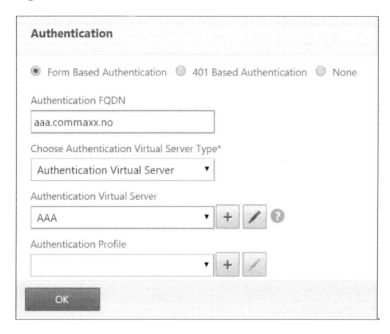

Click **OK** and then **Done**.

If we now try to browse the FQDN of the load-balanced vServer, we should be presented with a Citrix login webpage. After logging in with a LDAP based credential, we will be forwarded to the load-balanced servers.

 If we are having issues authenticating against an LDAP server, we can check the status for our authentication attempts under **Authentication | Logs** or we can use the command line to debug using the following commands:

```
shell
cd /tmp
cat aaad.deug
```

Another place to check for authentication attempts is on the security log on the particular LDAP/AD server.

Authorization policy

Now that we are done with a basic authentication policy, we can add an authorization policy which defines whether a client/user is allowed or denied access to a resource.

We can bind authorization policies to either:

- AAA users
- AAA groups
- Load balanced vServer
- Content Switching vServer

For this example, let us start with a policy that we bind to the same load balanced vServer and then create a new authorization policy that we bind to a particular AAA user.

Go into the **Security** | **AAA Application Traffic** | **Policies** | **Authorization**, then click on **Add**. Now let's say want to allow access to a particular range of IP-addresses. Start by giving the policy a name and choose the **Action** ALLOW. In the Expression field type enter CLIENT.IP.SRC.BETWEEN(192.168.0.0,192.168.0.5).

After we are done, click **OK**. Now we need to bind the authorization rule to a vServer. Go into the same load balanced vServer that we used earlier for AAA authentication and click on the **Policies** pane. Click the **+** sign, choose add authorization policy, and select the one we just created.

Now we try to open up a web browser and again go to the FQDN of the load balanced vServer. If we have a client computer that resides within that IP-address range, we will be allowed access to the resource after we have authenticated. It is important to note that authorization policies are processed after authentication policies. This is because we might have authorization rules that are attached to an AAA user or group, which can only be processed after a user has authenticated.

Now let's say that we want to allow access for a particular AAA user, even though he is outside that IP-range. What we first need to do is create an AAA user; this can be done under **AAA** | **Users**. From there click **Add**. Then enter the username of the LDAP user and click **OK**.

Now we have four options that we can bind to that user:

- AAA groups
- Authorization policies
- Session policies
- Audit policies

We will start by adding an authorization policy directly to that user. Click on the **Authorization Policy** pane and create a new policy. Choose the action `ALLOW` and in the expression field type `ns_true`; this is because we want that particular user to have access, since the default authorization rule is deny.

We can also define a more granular-based access, for instance if we wish to deny access to PDF files accessed via our load-balanced vServer.

Then we can create a new authorization policy, set the action to deny, and enter the expression:

`HTTP.REQ.URL.SUFFIX.EQ("pdf")`

After we are done with creating the policy, we need to bind it to the vServer. If for instance we have a user who is allowed access via an authorization policy, the user will still not be able to access PDF files since the strictest rules always win.

But this policy will only trigger when the URL suffix is PDF, so the user will still be able to open other file types on the same service.

Authentication profiles

Now by default we can use the same AAA vServer and attach it to many different vServers. When a user authenticates to one of these resources, the user is also given access to the other resources since he has already authenticated. In some cases, we might need to define different security levels to our services—for instance, if we require two-factor authentication to access some certain services, or if we just want another level of authentication in order to access the service.

This can be done using authentication profiles. Within an authentication profile we can define what level of access a user is given after they authenticate. We can also define which domain the user is given access to.

Authentication profiles can be created by clicking on **Add** under **AAA | Authentication Profile**.

From here we need to enter a name for the profile and the FQDN of the AAA vServer. Then choose the AAA vServer we want to redirect authentication to and enter the important bits: the **Authentication Domain** and **Authentication Level**.

These are both optional settings, but can provide better security for published services. For instance, if I have an authentication profile with an authentication domain, when a user authenticates the browser will get a session cookie with the domain name set. Therefore if I have other resources which I publish using the same domain, the user is automatically allowed in. If I set up resources using another domain, the user will need to re-authenticate. The authentication level also provides greater security; for instance, if we have an authentication profile with the security level set to 2, users who are authenticated are only allowed to access resources that have the same security level or lower. This means that, if a user tries to access a resource behind a security level of 1, he/she will need to re-authenticate. So let's follow this as an example.

We have two web services we want to publish with external authentication. One of the services is accessible for all users and will therefore be given a security level of 5; the other service is only available for users who authenticate using 2-factor authentication, and therefore will be given a security level of 1.

First we need to have two load-balanced vServers in place that present the two web services. Next we need to create two authentication profiles. In order to make this example simple, we will be using the same AAA vServer. The best approach would be to have two AAA vServers, where one of them has a simple LDAP policy bound and the other has LDAP and RADIUS for 2-factor authentication.

So we can start by creating a simple authentication profile for all external users. This should look like the following screenshot:

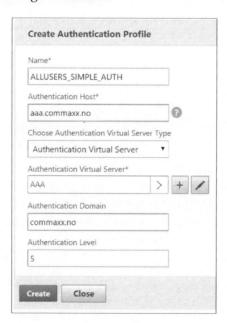

Then we create the other authentication profile, which looks the same except that we change the security level to 1 and change the profile name.

After we are done creating both profiles, we need to bind them to the load balanced vServers.

When binding them to the vServer, it is important that we choose the authentication profile instead of the authentication vServer, since the AAA vServer is already referenced in the profile.

We bind the one with the highest number (5) of security levels to the vServer for all users, and we bind the other with the lowest number (1) to the other service where we want better security.

We will notice now that, if we try to authenticate first to the vServer that has the authentication profile for all external users, we will be granted access. If we try to change the URL to the other vServer, we will be given a new login page again since we do not have the right security level.

Troubleshooting AAA and setting up audit policies

In some cases, it might be necessary to troubleshoot an AAA policy that is not correctly configured or if some users are having issues accessing certain services. This might be challenging as well because of the different mix of many authentication and authorization policies and the combination of users and different groups.

So where can we start to troubleshoot?

First off, the AAA feature has a monitor that allows us to see active user sessions. This can be viewed under **AAA | Active User Sessions** and lists all users who currently have an active session against NetScaler using the AAA module or even using ICA. In this view we can see if a user has successfully authenticated and is able to access a service.

If a user is not able to authenticate, we might need to start the `aaad.debug` feature within CLI to be able to pinpoint the authentication process. Another possibility might be running a trace during the authentication process; if we are using regular LDAP-based authentication, we can see the LDAP traffic using (for instance) Wireshark.

Another option might be to look inside the **Security Log** on the particular domain controller that is being used for authentication.

Another good idea is to check if the user has an active account in the domain; this can be checked from any computer that is part of the domain using the command:

```
net user /domain username
```

We can also enable AAA enhanced authentication feedback, which will tell the user in more detail what the issue might be if they are having problems authenticating.

This can only be set on a global level, and is applicable for both AAA-TM sessions and NetScaler Gateway sessions. It can be activated using this CLI command:

```
set aaa param -enableEnhancedAuthFeedBack
```

Or it can be activated by using the GUI by going into **NetScaler Gateway | Global Settings | Change authentication AAA settings** and enabling it from there.

When a user tries to logon and fails, the user can get one of the following error codes:

- **4001 - Invalid credentials. Catch-all error from previous versions**
- **4002 - Login not permitted. Catch-all error from previous versions**
- **4003 - Server timeout**
- **4004 - System error**
- **4005 - Socket error talking to authentication server**
- **4006 - Bad (format) user passed to nsaaad**
- **4007 - Bad (format) password passed to nsaaad**
- **4008 - Password mismatch (when entering new password)**
- **4009 - User not found**
- **4010 - Restricted login hours**
- **4011 - Account disabled**
- **4012 - Password expired**
- **4013 - No dial-in permission (RADIUS specific)**
- **4014 - Error changing password**
- **4015 - Account locked**

Summary

In this chapter we took a closer look at the different security features in NetScaler and some of the best practices with regard to management access and securing specific service traffic.

We also took a closer look at Citrix Insight Services and how we can use it to troubleshoot. Finally, we explored AAA and how we can use it to publish services with an authentication process.

In the last chapter we will take a closer look at various real-world deployments and how they might look from a technical perspective.

7
Real-World Deployment Scenarios

The purpose of many Citrix NetScaler environments is to provide load balancing, high availability for services, security, and authentication or remote access for Citrix XenApp/XenDesktop. Citrix NetScaler is one of the best application delivery controllers, and it is perfectly capable of different implementation scenarios. In this chapter, we will describe the most commonly used deployment scenarios. This chapter will inform you which configuration needs to be made to get this working. The deployment scenarios that we will describe are:

- A small PoC VDI environment
- An enterprise VDI multisite environment
- A global web services environment
- An active-active data center for application hosting
- An active-passive data center for disaster recovery
- Reverse proxy

A small PoC VDI environment

First of all, let's start what we and Citrix actually mean by **Proof of Concept (PoC)**. When we are implementing a PoC environment, we want to provide the customer with an opportunity to "test drive" the core processes in order to validate that their needs are met as expected.

A PoC should answer the following questions:

- Will the technology meet our needs?
- Will the product perform as advertised?
- Will the prospective end user be productive with the new way of doing this?
- Will the ultimate solution be feasible?

These questions need to be answered to determine whether a PoC has succeeded.

Besides a proof of concept, we also have a pilot environment. A pilot environment is an almost production-ready environment.

The following differences need to be kept in mind while choosing the right name for the right project:

	Proof of concept	Pilot
Goal	Proving the possibility of a solution or a critical aspect of a solution.	The first step towards a production deployment
Scope	Very specific. Provide the evaluation of customer-specific test cased.	Must consider all production environments
Cost	Free.	Fee
Environment capacity	Minimal (less than 10).	Smaller of 100 users or 10 percent of eventual users
Licenses purchased	Trail or limited.	Purchased
High availability	None.	Limited
Time to value	Short.	Medium to long
User interaction	Users test and provide direct feedback if the success criteria are fulfilled.	Users perform the function and a detailed level of feedback is collected

The preceding table displays the difference in how Citrix defines a PoC and a pilot environment.

So, when implementing a Citrix NetScaler as a proof of concept, we only install the Citrix NetScaler VPX with a free or a trail license. If we want to use Citrix NetScaler as ICA Proxy only, then we can use the NetScaler Gateway trail license as well. Because a proof of concept normally contains only one Citrix StoreFront server, we don't need the load balancing feature.

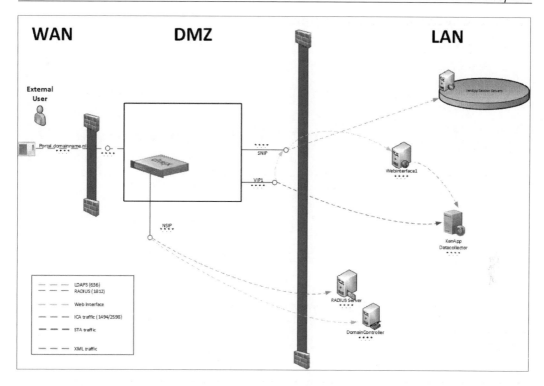

The preceding diagram shows a small VDI PoC environment with one Citrix NetScaler VPX Free/Trail, one Citrix StoreFront/Citrix WebInterface, and one Citrix XenApp/XenDesktop server. Also, the environment has a connection with one domain controller and one optional RADIUS server for two-factor authentication.

In most cases, the time in a proof of concept will not be paid. That's why only the necessary configuration will be made. Because the implementation hours will not get paid, we need to be sure that the prerequisite elements for the Citrix NetScaler Proof of Concept are ready before implementation:

- Get the proper license
- Get the network topology
- Get the network routes
- Get the IP address (NSIP/SNIP/VIP)
- Get the necessary SSL certificates
- Get information about the Citrix environment

- Get the Active Directory information and the service account

- Get the IP address and the secret key from the RADIUS server

- The firewall rules need to configured so that traffic can flow between the DMZ and the LAN networks

An enterprise VDI multisite environment

Nowadays, in a lot of companies, the IT environment is way more important than it was a few years ago. The IT environment is one of the primary processes. For example, the order system or the e-mails need to be fully functional 24 hours a day, 7 days a week. This makes it hard for the IT department to perform maintenance or migrations, for example.

Because of this, companies need to invest more money in the IT environment to make sure that it is fully functional at any time, for example, with data centers at different locations. This data center could be on the other side of the building or at a separate location. This separated location could be a colocation provider, for example.

When implementing a second or a third data center, we also need to be aware of the changes that need to be made to the environment. All data centers need to be connected with each other through a good connection with a high capacity to transfer data between the data center locations.

Also, we need to think about whether the secondary data center will be in an active/active configuration or an active/passive configuration. In an active/active configuration, it's possible to let users connect to both data centers. In active/passive mode, only one data center will be available for the user; if the current active data center stops running, the IT department can switch over to the passive data center.

Depending on the needs and the available finances, we need to consider whether the IT environment should be in active/active or active/passive mode. Also, between the active/passive functionality we can make a difference. This is because it's possible to have the passive data center start up automatically when the primary data center stops running.

Normally, the storage will always be in an active/active configuration. This is because if the active data center stops running, we don't like to use old data when running on the passive data center.

When we have an active/active data center or an active/passive data center with automatic failover, we need to think about whether the users have a connection to the environment. In the case of Citrix, all users are connected through Citrix StoreFront or the Citrix NetScaler Gateway functionality. The user connects through the Citrix Receiver or through a web browser to the environment. So basically, the user is connecting through HTTP or HTTPs traffic to a **Fully Qualified Domain Name (FQDN)**. This FQDN will be translated by the DNS server into an IP address. In the case of an active/active data center configuration, or when the environment is configured with different IP addresses, we need at least two IP addresses available for Citrix StoreFront and Citrix NetScaler Gateway in every data center.

Because of these different IP addresses, users don't know how to connect should there be a problem. The GSLB functionality can help us with this issue. With GSLB, we can use different IP addresses; if there is a problem, the GSLB functionality recognizes this and disables one of the IP addresses.

In the next diagram, we can find an active/active Citrix environment configuration based on the Citrix NetScaler Enterprise or Platinum license. In this configuration, we're using Citrix NetScaler to determine whether the user is logging in.

Global server load balancing is configured on the fastest response time, which means that the fastest data center will respond to the user.

In every data center, we're using Citrix NetScaler to load balance Citrix StoreFront, the Citrix Data Collectors, and the Active Directory with failover to the other data center. These failover virtual servers will be used only if the servers in their own data center stop running. This ensures that there is no single point of failure.

As discussed in *Chapter 1, Configuring the Standard Features of NetScaler®*, we need to perform a callback from the Citrix StoreFront server to Citrix NetScaler. When using GSLB, it could be possible that the callback functionality is sent to the other data center.

To arrange this, we're installing a separate Citrix NetScaler Gateway virtual server; it will be used only for the callback. This ensures that always the correct Citrix NetScaler Gateway will be contacted. This Citrix NetScaler Gateway virtual server for callback needs a separate URL, for example, `dc1-citrix.company.com`.

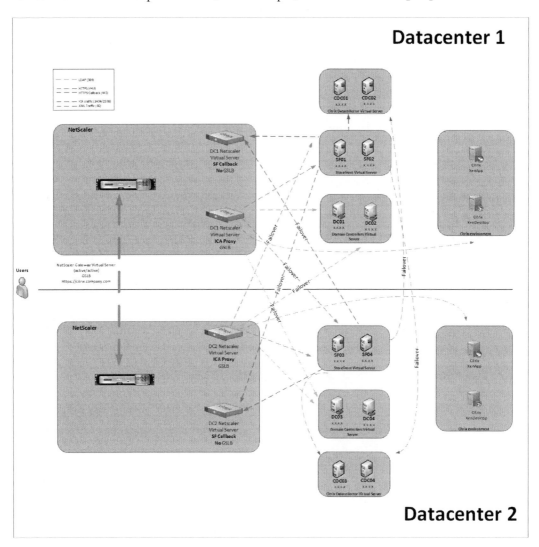

The Citrix StoreFront environment will be configured as a separated server group per data center. We're creating separated server groups per data center because we need to make some adjustments to each data center to ensure some settings. As server farms in Citrix StoreFront, we will create two farms, one per data center. Since the same applications/desktops are running in both data centers, we will see all the appliances double; this is because we're searching in two server farms. With a little adjustment from Citrix StoreFront, we will display only the primary server farm (the Citrix environment) in its own data center. This customization needs to be done on all the Citrix StoreFront servers manually.

The following configuration items will be used:

- There are two separate data centers with separate and independent XenDesktop sites on each data center: Datacenter 1, and Datacenter 2.

- There is a Citrix NetScaler Enterprise or Platinum on each data center with GSLB, where Citrix NetScaler is configured as authoritative for a GSLB subdomain.

- Three Citrix NetScaler Gateway GSLB virtual servers are configured as follows in each data center:

    ◦ `citrix.company.com`: This is the Citrix NetScaler GSLB virtual server that provides the FQDN that users enter in their browser in order to locate their desktops or applications. This URL is configured for active/active GSLB across both datacenters. Load balancing will be based on health monitoring and fastest response time.

    ◦ `datacenter1-citrix.company.com`: This is a Citrix NetScaler Gateway virtual server that refers to the Citrix NetScaler Gateway virtual server hosted in Datacenter 1. This virtual server will be used for ICA Proxy traffic to Datacenter 1. It will be configured in an active/passive GSLB configuration, where traffic will only be routed to Datacenter 2 in the event that Datacenter 1 is inaccessible.

    ◦ `datacenter2-citrix.company.com`: This is a Citrix NetScaler Gateway virtual server that refers to the Citrix NetScaler Gateway virtual server hosted in Datacenter 2. This Citrix NetScaler Gateway virtual server will be used for ICA Proxy traffic to Datacenter 2. It will be configured in an active/passive GSLB configuration, where traffic will only be routed to Datacenter 1 in the event that Datacenter 2 is inaccessible.

- Besides the Citrix NetScaler Gateway virtual server where the user actually connects, we need an additional Citrix NetScaler Gateway virtual server in each data center. This will be used for callback authentication from Citrix StoreFront to the Citrix NetScaler Gateway. Because the callback authentication must go back to the original Citrix NetScaler Gateway, we need a separate Citrix NetScaler Gateway virtual server that will not be used in the GSLB configuration:

  ° `datacenter1-callback.company.com` (Citrix NetScaler Gateway virtual server in Datacenter 1)

  ° `datacenter2-callback.company.com` (Citrix NetScaler Gateway virtual server in Datacenter 2)

- At least one pair of Citrix StoreFront servers at each data center:

  ° Multiple Citrix NetScaler load balancing virtual servers will be created to provide access to the Citrix StoreFront servers. The Citrix StoreFront load balancing virtual servers will use the other data center as a failover virtual server.

- At least one Citrix XenApp/XenDesktop site per data center.

Citrix® StoreFront™ multisite configuration

In order to let Citrix StoreFront run in a multisite configuration, we need to adjust `web.config` in the `C:\inetpub\wwwroot\Citrix\storename\` directory, where `storename` is the name specified for the store when it was created.

These adjustments can't be made through the GUI because they are not implemented yet. To ensure that the user sees the published applications and desktops from only one data center, the published applications and desktops will become visible only when the primary data centers closest to the data center are not able to host Citrix XenApp/XenDesktop sessions.

Search for this code in `web.config`:

```
<resourcesWingConfigurations>
  <resourcesWingConfiguration name="Default" wingName="Default" />
</resourcesWingConfigurations>
```

Change it to the following:

```
<resourcesWingConfigurations>
  <resourcesWingConfiguration name="Default" wingName="Default">
    <userFarmMappings>
      <clear />
```

```
<userFarmMapping name="user_mapping">
  <groups>
    <group name="domain\usergroup" sid="securityidentifier"
/>
    <group ... />
    ...
  </groups>
  <equivalentFarmSets>
    <equivalentFarmSet name="setname"
loadBalanceMode="{LoadBalanced | Failover}"
      aggregationGroup="aggregationgroupname">
      <primaryFarmRefs>
        <farm name="primaryfarmname" />
      </primaryFarmRefs>
      <backupFarmRefs>
        <farm name="backupfarmname" />
      </backupFarmRefs>
    </equivalentFarmSet>
  </equivalentFarmSets>
</userFarmMapping>

    </userFarmMappings>
  </resourcesWingConfiguration>
</resourcesWingConfigurations>
```

The new `web.config` contains some new features that make it possible to have a multisite configuration. The parameters that are highlighted need to be filled in and can be found here:

- `userFarmMapping`: In this section, we can configure the users to access for this type of deployment. It controls user access to resources by using the Microsoft Active Directory user groups to the specified groups of deployments. Normally, this would be the Domain Users group.

- `groups`: This is the same as `userFarmMapping`, but here the names and **security identifiers (SIDs)** of Active Directory user groups will be used. Make sure that the username is entered in the domain/usergroup format.

- `equivalentFarmSet`: The `equivalentFarmSet` contains the actual information that Citrix StoreFront uses to configure the multisite configuration. The `loadBalanceMode` determines the allocation of users in the deployment configuration. When the value is set to `LoadBalanced`, Citrix StoreFront distributes users across all the available deployments. When the value is set to `Failover`, users are connected to the first available deployment in the order in which they are listed in the configuration.

Set the value of the `loadBalanceMode` attribute to `LoadBalanced` to randomly assign users to deployments in the equivalent deployment set, evenly distributing users across all the available deployments. When the value of the `loadBalanceMode` attribute is set to `Failover`, users are connected to the first available deployment in the order in which they are listed in the configuration, minimizing the number of deployments in use at any given time.

- `primaryFarmRefs`: This value will contain the farm of the primary farm configured in Citrix StoreFront. The name or names that will be used as the primary farm need to exactly match the names that we entered in the Citrix StoreFront configuration.

- `backupFarmRefs`: This value contains the secondary farm configured in Citrix StoreFront. This `backpFarmRefs` value will be used only when the primary farm doesn't respond anymore.

Citrix® StoreFront™ optimal NetScaler Gateway™ routing

To make sure that the Citrix StoreFront server uses the Citrix NetScaler Gateway that is in the same data center, we need to configure this in the `web.config` configuration file. So, this configuration contains information on which Citrix NetScaler Gateway should be used closest to the Citrix StoreFront server.

Search for the following code in `web.config`:

```
<optimalGatewayForFarmsCollection />
```

Change it to this:

```
<optimalGatewayForFarmsCollection>
  <optimalGatewayForFarms enabledOnDirectAccess="{true | false}">
    <farms>
      <farm name="farmname" />
    </farms>
    <optimalGateway key="_" name="deploymentname"
stasUseLoadBalancing="{true | false}"
      stasBypassDuration="hh:mm:ss" enableSessionReliability="{true
| false}"
      useTwoTickets="{true | false}">
      <hostnames>
        <add hostname="appliancefqdn:port" />
      </hostnames>
      <staUrls>
        <add staUrl="https://stapath/scripts/ctxsta.dll" />
```

```
        </staUrls>
      </optimalGateway>
    </optimalGatewayForFarms>
    <optimalGatewayForFarms>
      ...
    </optimalGatewayForFarms>
  </optimalGatewayForFarmsCollection>
```

The new `web.config` file contains some new features that make it possible to use the optimal Citrix NetScaler Gateway. The parameters that are highlighted need to be filled in and can be found here:

- `optimalGatewayForFarms`: Set the value of the `enabledOnDirectAccess` attribute to `true` to ensure that local users on the internal network log on to StoreFront directly. All the requested connections to their resources are routed through the optimal Citrix NetScaler Gateway appliance for the deployment. When the value of the `enabledOnDirectAccess` attribute is set to `false`, the connections to resources are not routed through the optimal Citrix NetScaler Gateway appliance unless users access StoreFront through the NetScaler Gateway.

- `farms`: This specifies the server farms that share a common optimal Citrix NetScaler Gateway appliance.

- `optimalGateway`: This specifies the configuration details of the optimal Citrix NetScaler Gateway appliance for users so as to access resources. Enter a name for the Citrix NetScaler Gateway appliance that helps you identify it.

  Set the value of the `stasUseLoadBalancing` attribute to `true` to randomly obtain session tickets from all STAs. When the value of the `stasUseLoadBalancing` attribute is set to `false`, users are connected to the first available STA in the order in which they are listed in the configuration. Use the `stasBypassDuration` attribute to set the time period for which an STA is considered unavailable after a failed request.

  To keep disconnected sessions open while Citrix Receiver attempts to reconnect automatically, set the value of the `enableSessionReliability` attribute to `true`. If we configure multiple STAs and want to ensure that session reliability is always available, we set the value of the `useTwoTickets` attribute to `true` to obtain session tickets from two different STAs just in case one STA becomes unavailable during the session.

- `hostnames`: This specifies the fully qualified domain name and port of the optimal NetScaler Gateway appliance.

- `staUrls`: This specifies the URLs for the Citrix XenDesktop or XenApp that runs the **Secure Ticket Authority (STA)** in the environment. Choose the STA closest matching in the Citrix StoreFront data center.

Citrix® StoreFront™ subscription synchronization

Citrix XenApp/XenDesktop users are able to subscribe to applications that they want to see as default. These subscriptions are stored in the database on the Citrix StoreFront servers. Because we will create a server group per data center, we need to make sure that the database will be synchronized between the data centers. This synchronization will make sure that all subscribed applications are visible in all data centers.

The subscription synchronization can be configured as follows:

1. Use an account with local administrator permissions, start PowerShell, and type the following commands to import the StoreFront modules:

    ```
    Import-Module "C:\Program Files\Citrix\Receiver StoreFront\
    Management\Cmdlets\UtilsModule.psm1"
    ```

    ```
    Import-Module "C:\Program Files\Citrix\Receiver StoreFront\
    Management\Cmdlets\SubscriptionSyncModule.psm1"
    ```

2. To specify the remote Citrix StoreFront deployment containing the store to be synchronized, type this command:

    ```
    Add-DSSubscriptionsRemoteSyncCluster –clusterName deploymentname
      –clusterAddress deploymentaddress
    ```

    Here, `deploymentname` is the name that helps identify the other data center, and `deploymentaddress` is the accessible address of the Citrix StoreFront server or Citrix NetScaler load balancing virtual server for the other data center.

3. To specify the store with which to synchronize users' application subscriptions, type the following command:

    ```
    Add-DSSubscriptionsRemoteSyncStore –clusterName deploymentname
      –storeName storename
    ```

    Here, `deploymentname` is the name that helps identify the other data center, and `storeName` is the name specified for both the local and remote stores when they were created.

4. To configure regular synchronization at specific intervals, type this command:

    ```
    Add-DSSubscriptionsSyncReoccuringSchedule –scheduleName
      synchronizationname –startTime hh:mm:ss -repeatMinutes interval
    ```

Here, `synchronizationname` is a name that helps identify the schedule that we're creating. Use the `-startTime` setting to specify the delay in hours, minutes, and seconds before the new schedule becomes active. For the interval option, specify the time in minutes between each synchronization in the `repeatMinutes` value.

5. Add the domain machine accounts from all Citrix StoreFront servers in the remote deployment to the local Windows user group called `CitrixSubscriptionSyncUsers` on the current Citrix StoreFront server.

6. If the Citrix StoreFront deployment consists of multiple servers per data center, use the Citrix StoreFront management console to propagate the configuration changes to other servers in the server group.

7. Repeat steps 1 to 6 on the remote StoreFront deployment to configure a subscription synchronization schedule from the remote deployment to the local deployment.

8. To start synchronizing application subscriptions between the stores by restarting subscriptions, store the service on both the local and remote deployments. At a Windows PowerShell Command Prompt on a server in each deployment, type the following command:

```
Restart-DSSubscriptionsStoreSubscriptionService
```

An enterprise VDI active-passive environment

Besides the multisite environment (which is in active/active mode), it is also possible to configure Citrix NetScaler and the required resources based on active/passive mode.

If there is a stretched VLAN between data centers, then we can use the Citrix NetScaler high availability mode. This mode is in the Citrix NetScaler Standard license. The stretched VLAN technique allows us to use the same IP addresses in both data centers. If you choose high availability mode, then the adjustments for the Citrix StoreFront multisite and optimal NetScaler Gateway aren't necessary.

If there is no stretched VLAN available, then we can use the global server load balancing functionality in Citrix NetScaler. This allows us to create a backup virtual server with another IP configuration, which will become active when the active data center stops working. If the primary data center comes back online, we can set it as the active data center again, which ensures that all the users will connect through the active data center.

In the event of a failover, Citrix NetScaler will use the passive data center, so users will get a Citrix session on the passive data center. Please be aware when switching back to the active data center that users will lose their Citrix session when there is no stretched VLAN and Citrix NetScaler can't reach the other data center.

A global web services environment

Citrix NetScaler is capable of implementing a global web services environment, especially when using the content switching feature. This feature is available from the Citrix NetScaler Free and higher licenses. With the content switching feature, we can use only one WAN IP address for different backend servers. In this way, we can consolidate WAN IP addresses.

If you are using a lot of secure traffic, it's better to use a physical Citrix NetScaler MPX or SDX because of the hardware SSL chip. Besides the SSL chip, please be aware of the generated HTTP requests per second. This number of requests per second is necessary to determine the most suitable hardware for the environment.

When a web service is based on a lot of static website information, we should consider using application acceleration, application security, and frontend optimization. All of these features give a guarantee that the environment is ready to deliver the best performance for every device, and protect the environment.

Application acceleration will be used to cache from pages whenever possible. This will ensure that the pages that are requested by users more often will get the page from Citrix NetScaler instead of the web server at the backend. This offloads the backend web server.

Nowadays, Distributed Denial of Service (DDoS) is very hot item. This is because a lot of environments are getting DDoS attacks. Citrix NetScaler is capable of preventing these kinds of attacks.

With frontend optimization, we can optimize traffic for different devices. For example, we can convert GIF images to PNG, optimize JPEG files by removing non-image data, optimize CSS files, and so on. This optimization will ensure that websites can be loaded fast from every type of device and connection.

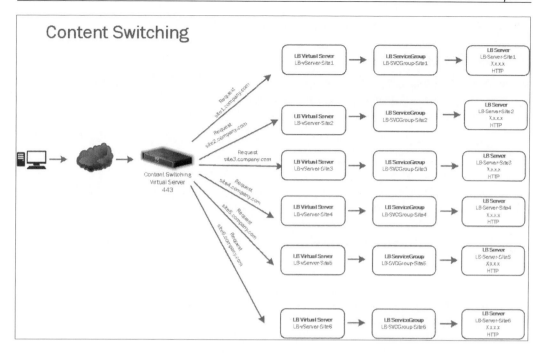

As we can see in the preceding figure, we're using only that IP address that needs to be available from the public Internet. Based on the expression, we can define to which load balancing virtual server the Citrix NetScaler content switching should connect.

To have a trusted and secure connection, it's best to use a secure connection based on **443** when the web service needs this. The Citrix NetScaler content switching supports the SNI feature. With the SNI feature, we can to bind multiple certificates. We can specify subdomains in this feature too. Internally, the Citrix NetScaler appliance parses the certificates and extracts the domain names. Citrix NetScaler stores these domain names in a hash table.

So, for global web services, it's better to use the Citrix NetScaler Platinum Edition based on a physical appliance. This edition allows us to use all the necessary features that leverage quality and speed for the web service environment.

An active-active data center for application hosting

Citrix NetScaler has support for active/active data centers for the purpose of application hosting. The active/active solution can be done in two different ways depending on the WAN connection.

An active/active data center solution for application hosting can be done by using global server load balancing or the Citrix NetScaler clustering feature. For both features, the Enterprise license is required.

During implementation, we need to define which feature suits the best for the company. If the company has only one Internet link for both data centers, then probably global server load balancing won't help with anything. In this particular case, we recommend the use of the Citrix NetScaler clustering feature. The Citrix NetScaler clustering feature allows us to bind up to 32 Citrix NetScaler appliances with each other. By creating a cluster, we can use all the nodes as one active device. This ensures high performance across different data centers.

For application hosting, we need the reserve proxy feature in the Citrix NetScaler. The reserve proxy is called load balancing in the Citrix NetScaler. Because application hosting will need a lot of external WAN IP addresses, we can use the content switching feature in front of the load balancing services as well. So basically, it is the same setup as the global web services, only with the Citrix NetScaler clustering feature in front of it.

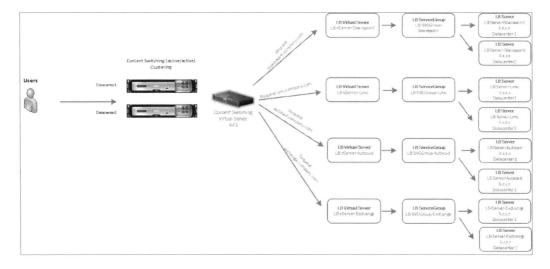

The preceding figure describes the configuration of a NetScaler clustering feature in combination with application hosting services. As you can see, there are two Citrix NetScaler appliances configured, both in different data centers. Because they are in clustering mode, they share the same configuration. This means that we can't match the backend resources to the nearest Citrix NetScaler appliance. So, it could be possible that the Citrix NetScaler appliance in Datacenter 1 is gathering data from the backend server in the other data center. In this scenario, there should be a stretched VLAN between the data centers, because the appliances have to reach each other.

When the company has more WAN connections available, or when there is no stretched VLAN between the data centers, we need to use global server load balancing to get support for this functionality. This allows us to have separate connections between both data centers—by the WAN and LAN connections.

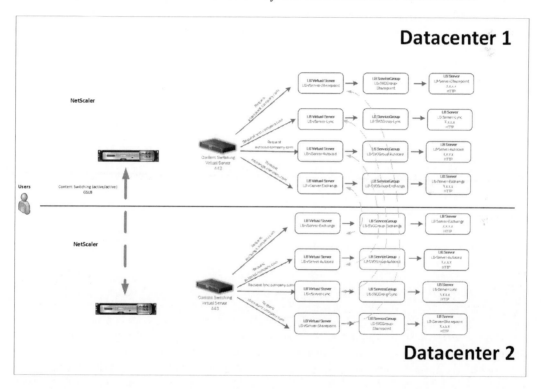

Using GSLB in combination with content switching allows us to use the closest backend services that match the same geographic location of the Citrix NetScaler appliance.

An active-passive data center for disaster recovery

The best configuration for Citrix NetScaler in an active-passive data center for disaster recovery is by using the global server load balancing feature for all resources that need to be accessed in the event of a failover to the passive data center.

But a standard high availability would fit this scenario as well when the backend environment has the same setup as the active data center. This means that there are no servers active in the passive data center. The servers will become active only when the active data center stops working. The servers in the passive data center side will need to be started manually by the hypervisor environment.

To use the high availability feature on Citrix NetScaler instead of global server load balancing, we need to be sure that the servers are configured with the same configuration as in the active data center:

- Hostname
- IP address
- DNS server

So basically, the virtual machines in the active data center should be running in the passive data center if the active data center stops working.

If the server configuration in the passive data center is different from that in the active data center (for example, because it's a copy), then we should use the global server load balancing feature. This feature allows us to configure Citrix NetScaler with two different configurations for both data centers.

So, we need to configure a Citrix NetScaler Enterprise appliance in both data centers and configure these to match the configuration.

After this configuration, we're going to configure the global server load balancing virtual servers. During the configuration, we should configure the passive data center load balancing virtual servers as backup failover servers. This means that the passive data center will become active only if the active data center stops running.

The global server load balancing feature is especially useful when there are two or more data centers available with different configurations.

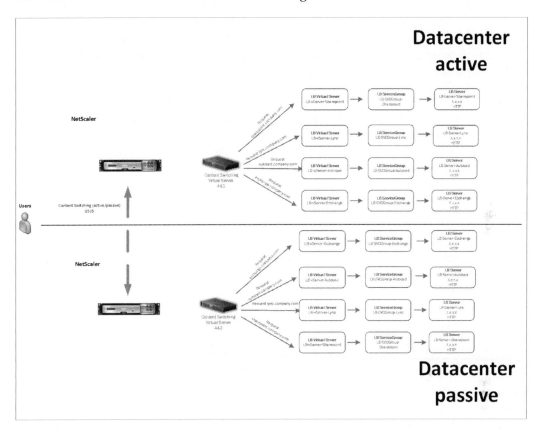

As you can see in the preceding figure, the configuration is almost the same as that of the active/active data center for application hosting and the active/passive enterprise VDI environment.

The only main difference between the active/active data center for application hosting and this scenario is the failover between the data centers configured on the load balancing virtual servers and the actually active/passive configuration of GSLB.

Reverse proxy

Nowadays, a lot of companies need to publish resources through the Internet. You can think about the e-mail environment, certain websites, customer relationship management, and so on. Citrix NetScaler can help companies arrange this using the reverse proxy methodology. Citrix NetScaler will be the proxy between the Internet and the company network. So basically, the servers can be in the LAN network and Citrix NetScaler will be placed in the DMZ zone. This will perform a secure connection.

With the reverse proxy functionality, it's also possible to perform a trusted and secure connection from outside by using an SSL certificate, and from Citrix NetScaler, this can be done using a single HTTP connection. This has an advantage; there is no change necessary on the server.

Lately, Citrix NetScaler has been used a lot for the reverse proxy functionality, because of the end-of-life from Microsoft TMG. Microsoft TMG was a reverse proxy that was used a lot for the Microsoft Exchange, SharePoint reverse proxy.

The use of reverse proxy and two separate connections makes it possible to use two different certificates when it is necessary. For example, the Microsoft Exchange environment requires a multi-domain certificate, because the certificate also needs the FQDN of the server (`exchange01.company.local`). But since November 1, 2015, it's not allowed to request a certificate with a local domain name included. While using Citrix NetScaler as reverse proxy, it's still possible to create a self-signed certificate or a certificate created by the Microsoft Certificate Authority in the domain environment. This self-signed or Microsoft Certificate Authority certificate will be installed on Citrix NetScaler and on the Microsoft Exchange Server. The public certificate, without the internal domain certificate, will be used from the Internet, and the internal certificate will be used to communicate from Citrix NetScaler to the Microsoft Exchange Server.

Using Citrix NetScaler as reverse proxy will allow the company to still use an internal domain name in the certificate for internal use and to changes needs to be made on the Microsoft Exchange environment.

Summary

We have now gone through some real-world deployment scenarios. These are the common scenarios right now, but you can imagine that there are a lot more available.

As we can see, the global server load balancing feature is a feature that fits best in all the scenarios. This is because the load balancing is based on DNS instead of IP addresses. This allows us to configure one DNS entry for both data centers per resource. Also, the user needs to remember one URL per resource instead of knowing the IP addresses of both data centers and figuring out which IP address is the active one.

In most scenarios, it's best to use a physical appliance because of the traffic that will flow through Citrix NetScaler.

Throughout this book, we have written the most common features that Citrix NetScaler has to offer. These features were explained as much as possible, but of course, not all information can fit in one book. So, if you are interested in learning more about the features of Citrix NetScaler and checking out news about it, we encourage you to visit the following websites and links:

- Citrix's blog about Citrix NetScaler: `http://blogs.citrix.com/product/netscaler`
- Citrix's blog about Citrix NetScaler Gateway: `http://blogs.citrix.com/product/netscaler-gateway`
- *Citrix Product Documentation*: `http://docs.citrix.com`
- *Netscaler Knowledgebase*: `http://www.NetScalerkb.com`
- Blog by author Marius Sandbu: `http://msandbu.wordpress.com`
- Blog by author Rick Roetenberg: `http://www.rickroetenberg.com`

Index

deployment modes, CloudBridge™
about 68
group mode 68
high-availability mode 68
inline mode 68
inline with dual bridges 68
redirector mode 68
transparent mode 68
virtual inline mode 68
WCCP mode 68
device discovery, Citrix® Command Center
about 78
process 79
device groups, Citrix® Command Center 78
device profiles, Citrix® Command Center 77
distributed agents, Citrix® Command
Center 76, 77
Distributed Denial-of-Service (DDoS)
attacks 42
DNS
about 92
adding 92-95

E

Endpoint Analysis (EPA) 27
enterprise VDI active-passive
environment 181
enterprise VDI multisite
environment 172-175
expressions
using 44, 45

F

filter options, nstcpdump
arp 130
dst port <Port_Number> 130
host <IP_Address> 130
icmp 130
net <Subnet_Address> mask
<Netmask> 130
port <Port_Number> 130
portrange <From_Port_Number>-
<To_Port_Number> 130
src port <Port_Number> 130
tcp 130
udp 130

Forward Acknowledgement (FACK) 119
Fully Qualified Domain Name (FQDN) 173

G

generic SQL load balancing
setting up 108, 109
GeoLite database
reference link 142
Global Server Load Balancing (GSLB)
about 95-100
components 95
purposes 95
troubleshooting 105-107
Global Server Load Balancing Site IP
Addresses (GSLBIPs) 3
global web services environment 182, 183
group policies 32

H

hardware appliances, Citrix® Command
Center 76
HDX Insight
about 57
reference link 57
high availability, Citrix® Command
Center 76
High Availability (HA) 78
HTTP/2 124, 125
HTTP Callouts
about 38
configuring 39-41
working 38, 39
HTTP DoS protection 150, 151

I

ICA 119
Insight deployment management 65
installation, CloudBridge™
about 70
compression 70
encrypted traffic acceleration 71
SSL compression 72
traffic shaping 73

NTP daemon
  configuring, URL 148

O

object identifier (OID) 79
optimal NetScaler Gateway™ routing,
  StoreFront 178, 179

P

parameters, nstrace
  -filesize 128
  -filter 128
  -mode 128
  -name 128
  -perNIC 128
  -tcpdump 127
  -time 127
policies
  evaluation order 46
  parsing 47
  reference link 45
  using 44, 45
policy binding 45, 46
port settings, Citrix® Command Center 78
prerequisites, Citrix NetScaler®
  cluster 59
  HA 59
  HDX Insight 59
  HTTP/HTTPS 59
  nCore 59
  NetScaler® State 59
  NSIP 59
  NS user 59
  NTP 59
  Standalone NetScaler Gateway™ 59
Proof of Concept (PoC) 169
protocol version 108

Q

Quality of Service (QoS) 66
Qualys SSL Labs
  URL 124

R

rate limiting
  about 42
  configuring 42, 43
Receiver for Web 31
Remote Method Invocation (RMI) 78
reporting, Citrix® Command Center 81
reporting, NetScaler® Insight Center
  about 57
  HDX Insight 57
  WAN Insight 58
  Web Insight 57
reports, for Web Insight
  applications 57
  devices 57
  domains 57
responder feature
  about 51
  versus rewrite feature 53
responder policy
  configuring 51, 52
reverse proxy 188
rewrite feature
  about 47
  actions 49
  GoTo expression 48
  versus responder feature 53
  working 47, 48
rewrite policy
  configuring 50, 51

S

Secure Sockets Layer (SSL) 47
Secure Ticket Authority (STA) 179
security features, NetScaler 149, 150
security identifiers (SIDs) 177
Selective Acknowledgement (SACK) 119
session policies 25-29
Simple Network Management Protocol
  (SNMP) 79
Single Sign On (SSO) 14
small PoC VDI environment 169-172
SmartAccess filters 33
software, Citrix® Command Center 75
SPDY 124, 125

Thank you for buying
Mastering NetScaler VPX™

About Packt Publishing

Packt, pronounced 'packed', published its first book, *Mastering phpMyAdmin for Effective MySQL Management*, in April 2004, and subsequently continued to specialize in publishing highly focused books on specific technologies and solutions.

Our books and publications share the experiences of your fellow IT professionals in adapting and customizing today's systems, applications, and frameworks. Our solution-based books give you the knowledge and power to customize the software and technologies you're using to get the job done. Packt books are more specific and less general than the IT books you have seen in the past. Our unique business model allows us to bring you more focused information, giving you more of what you need to know, and less of what you don't.

Packt is a modern yet unique publishing company that focuses on producing quality, cutting-edge books for communities of developers, administrators, and newbies alike. For more information, please visit our website at www.packtpub.com.

About Packt Enterprise

In 2010, Packt launched two new brands, Packt Enterprise and Packt Open Source, in order to continue its focus on specialization. This book is part of the Packt Enterprise brand, home to books published on enterprise software – software created by major vendors, including (but not limited to) IBM, Microsoft, and Oracle, often for use in other corporations. Its titles will offer information relevant to a range of users of this software, including administrators, developers, architects, and end users.

Writing for Packt

We welcome all inquiries from people who are interested in authoring. Book proposals should be sent to author@packtpub.com. If your book idea is still at an early stage and you would like to discuss it first before writing a formal book proposal, then please contact us; one of our commissioning editors will get in touch with you.

We're not just looking for published authors; if you have strong technical skills but no writing experience, our experienced editors can help you develop a writing career, or simply get some additional reward for your expertise.

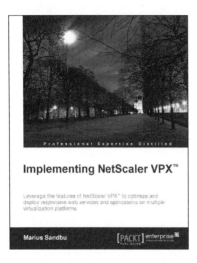

Implementing NetScaler VPX™

ISBN: 978-1-78217-267-3   Paperback: 136 pages

Leverage the features of NetScaler VPX™ to optimize and deploy responsive web services and applications on multiple virtualization platforms

1. Learn how to design, set up, and deploy Netscaler VPX in a virtual environment to make all your Web applications faster and secure.

2. Harness the power and efficiencies of off-the-shelf hardware and their virtualized, dynamic datacenters.

3. Step-by-step instructions showing you how to implement different features using sample scenarios and real-world examples.

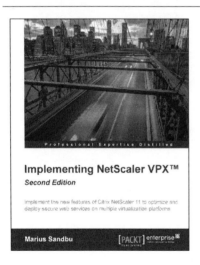

Implementing NetScaler VPX™
Second Edition

ISBN: 978-1-78528-898-2   Paperback: 202 pages

Implement the new features of Citrix NetScaler 11 to optimize and deploy secure web services on multiple virtualization platforms

1. Learn how to design, set up, and deploy NetScaler VPX along with the new Jumbo frames in a virtual environment using your GUI as well as your CLI for both public and private clouds to make all your web applications faster and more secure.

2. Enrich your networking skills utilizing the new features of AAA by following the instructions to optimize network traffic.

Please check **www.PacktPub.com** for information on our titles

Citrix® XenApp® 6.5 Expert Cookbook

ISBN: 978-1-84968-522-1   Paperback: 420 pages

Over 125 recipes that enable you to configure, administer, and troubleshoot a XenApp® infrastructure for effective application virtualization

1. Create installation scripts for Citrix XenApp, License Servers, Web Interface, and StoreFront.

2. Use PowerShell scripts to configure and administer the XenApp's infrastructure components.

3. Discover Citrix and community written tools to maintain a Citrix XenApp infrastructure.

Mastering Citrix® XenDesktop®

ISBN: 978-1-78439-397-7   Paperback: 484 pages

Design and implement a high performance and efficient virtual desktop infrastructure using Citrix® XenDesktop®

1. Design, deploy, configure, optimize, troubleshoot, and maintain XenDesktop for enterprise environments and to meet emerging high-end business requirements.

2. Configure Citrix XenDesktop to deliver a rich virtual desktop experience to end users.

3. A comprehensive, practical guide to monitoring a XenDesktop environment and automating XenDesktop tasks using PowerShell.

Please check **www.PacktPub.com** for information on our titles

Printed in Great Britain
by Amazon